Presidencies Derailed

Presidencies Derailed

Why University Leaders Fail and How to Prevent It

Stephen Joel Trachtenberg,
Gerald B. Kauvar,
and E. Grady Bogue

Johns Hopkins University Press
Baltimore

Johns Hopkins Paperback edition, 2016

9 8 7 6 5 4 3 2

Johns Hopkins University Press
2715 North Charles Street
Baltimore, Maryland 21218-4363
www.press.jhu.edu

The Library of Congress has cataloged the hardcover edition of this book as follows:

Trachtenberg, Stephen Joel.
    Presidencies derailed : why university leaders fail and how to prevent it /
Stephen Joel Trachtenberg, Gerald B. Kauvar, and E. Grady Bogue.
        pages   cm
    Includes bibliographical references and index.
    ISBN 978-1-4214-1024-1 (hardcover : alk. paper) — ISBN 978-1-4214-1025-8
(electronic) — ISBN 10421401024-9 (hardcover : alk. paper) — ISBN 1-4214-
1025-7 (electronic) 1. College presidents. 2. Universities and colleges—Administration. I. Title.
    LB2341.T6815 2013
    378.1'11—dc23   2012045838

A catalog record for this book is available from the British Library.

ISBN-13: 978-1-4214-1987-9
ISBN-10: 1-4214-1987-4

*Special discounts are available for bulk purchases of this book. For more informa-
tion, please contact Special Sales at 410-516-6936 or specialsales@press.jhu.edu.*

Contents

Preface   *vii*

Acknowledgments   *xiii*

1   Themes of Presidential Derailment   1

PART I: PRESIDENTS OFF-TRACK

2   Presidential Derailments at Private Liberal
     Arts Institutions   21
     Jason McNeal

3   Presidential Derailments at Public Master's
     Level Institutions   35
     Julie Longmire

4   Presidential Derailments at Public Research Universities   50
     Keith Carver

5   Presidential Derailments at Community Colleges   60
     Leigh Ann Touzeau

6   Firsthand Experiences of Derailed Presidents   71

PART II: AVERTING THE TRAIN WRECK

7   The Upstream Solution: More Thoughtful
     Academic Searches   97

8   Board Dynamics: A Piece of the Presidential
     Derailment Puzzle   111

9   Lessons Learned about Presidential Derailments   129

Appendix: A Year of Presidential Turnover   141

Bibliography   153

Contributors   155

Index   159

Preface

A derailed presidency can undermine an institution's image, destroy campus morale, and cost millions of dollars. We define a derailment as the termination or resignation of a president before the end of his or her first contract. We chose to focus on first-term derailments because they are all too frequent and represent a failure in the processes used to recruit, select, on-board, and nurture new presidents. During 2009 and 2010, fifty college, university, and system presidents resigned, retired prematurely, or were fired. They came from every type of institution (public, independent, and proprietary) and every level of experience. We detail many of these stories in the appendix.

This book attempts to understand what goes wrong and who in academic institutions has the responsibility to address issues before situations irreparably deteriorate. When we are able to uncover the details of a derailment, the lessons we learn may guide the feet of future college, university, and system leaders. However, more often than not, the details are impossibly obscured.

What We Know and Don't Know about Derailments

When presidents leave in turmoil, the negotiated settlement almost universally includes a confidentiality agreement, and troubled boards and academic administrations usually erect a wall of silence, preventing outsiders from determining what happened. Neither board members nor the derailed president wants the details of the failure or the cost of the settlement paraded through the press. The institution needs to move on from the crisis. The ex-president needs to get on with his or her professional life. In the immediate aftermath of a presidential derailment, full public disclosure appears in no one's best interest.

Years after the fact, the lessons we could learn from presidential derailments often remain cloaked. Media reports provide incomplete and sometimes misleading information. We are grateful that the individuals included in this book were willing to be forthright about their experiences. To protect their anonymity, their names and details about the institutions have been disguised. Many of the parties we would have liked to include in this publication were either unwilling to risk talking to us or were bound to silence by nondisclosure agreements.

In corporate life, in the military, in government, and in institutions of higher education, too many leadership derailments are attributable to easily identifiable failures—self-aggrandizement, arrogance, and aloofness. Despite abundant examples of how such behaviors led to derailment, leaders in the public eye continue to demonstrate similar failings. Leaders cheat on their spouses; they accept bribes in exchange for influence; they pad payrolls with relatives and incompetent cronies; they encourage kickbacks from vendors and accept personal services from institutional contractors; they browbeat subordinates; they deviate from the truth on financial disclosure forms and on their taxes. When caught, they often deny.

It's fair to ask why this occurs but hard to answer. Observers tend to agree that a bloated sense of entitlement is common, but it is not clear whether those unfortunate characteristics were exhibited in prior jobs. If so, the vetting undertaken during the search was perhaps insufficient. If not, and the president grew into the misbehaviors, the board and the president's cabinet share responsibility for not trying to nip the excesses in the bud. We hope that this book, in some small measure, offers a peek behind the curtain of presidential derailments. We have deliberately omitted some of the more prominent derailments and so-called scandals. A list of "collegiate scandals" that claimed the jobs of college presidents may be found in Daniel de Vise's blog "Eight Scandals That Ended College Presidencies" (de Vise 2011).

Drawing Lessons Learned

This book dramatizes sixteen case studies that illuminate and humanize a relatively small number of derailment themes and also provides firsthand accounts of two derailments and summaries of still others. "Derailment themes" is the language conventionally used in the literature on corporate executive derailment and in the methodological world of qualitative research. The themes found in higher education are, at best, associated with derailment generally. But, it would be a stretch to argue that they were the reasons or causes for any particular derailment. The roots of derailments are fibrous, not tap. These sixteen case studies reveal certain patterns: Derailments happen throughout the academy. Seasoned leaders and new administrators alike stumble. No one type or size of institution is immune. People are people; institutions are institutions.

From these case studies, we also conclude that prevention, while not necessarily difficult, requires concerted effort. When we began this effort, we thought we could put suggestions into categories of stakeholders—board members, search committees, and search firms. Given the intricate dance of an academic presidency, that assumption was misinformed. For example, more frequent and more structured evaluation of an incumbent's performance requires agreement between the incumbent and the board, not only on goals and objectives but also on timing and transparency. Likewise, a governance assessment will be useful to the board before it begins a search and to the president after the announcement, but it does not address underlying issues of board performance. Crafting less generic job announcements requires cooperation and a common understanding of the institution's current state and foreseeable future, as well as its aspirations.

This book provides a menu of best practices designed to forestall, if not prevent, future derailments. We offer recommendations for boards, for search committees, for executive search firms, and for legislators and governors to consider and adopt. It is our hope that the lessons learned from the derailments we studied may help prevent at least some similar losses in the future.

Reading between the Lines

As board members, presidents, and search firms, we walk into the middle of a story about institutional needs, leadership priorities, and specific circumstances. The chapters in this book need not be read sequentially, though the order makes sense. In chapter 1, we begin by looking at two sides of the leadership coin—effectiveness and failure. Our research and experience convinces us (and, we hope, you) that six identifiable themes presage derailments:

1. Ethical lapses, ranging from lavish spending to limited information sharing
2. Poor interpersonal skills, such as arrogant attitudes, volatile tempers, and weak communication skills
3. Inability to lead key constituencies, including board members, government officials, cabinet members, and faculty
4. Difficulty adapting to institutional culture, community context, or the academic presidency

5. Failure to meet business objectives, such as financial goals, fundraising expectations, and enrollment projections
6. Board shortcomings, from flawed search processes to dysfunctional board dynamics to conflicts of interest

Chapters 2 through 5 provide detailed studies of derailments within different types of institutions—liberal arts colleges, master's level institutions, comprehensive research universities, and community colleges. Each chapter includes four case studies based on real examples of presidential derailments. These four chapters present the candid and unvarnished comments of presidents, former presidents, other administrators, and board members and provide a personal texture to our analyses of derailments. While most derailments are shrouded in confidentiality agreements, the chapter authors were able to pierce the veil of secrecy by assuring participants in their studies absolute confidentiality. The events and views recounted are those of the participants. Their names, and those of their institutions, have been obscured in order to protect the innocent and the not-so-innocent.

In chapter 6, two derailed presidents agreed to contribute firsthand accounts for this volume. Their commentaries differ widely, but each account further illuminates the major derailment themes. Each is an example of personal advocacy, telling one side of a complex narrative. No doubt, as in the Kurasowa film *Rashomon*, each participant has his or her own version of the tale. By design, we want to offer thoughtful readers a distinct and distinctive perspective on the circumstances of identifiable and very public derailments. Those in search of Truth must consult the philosophy or religion departments.

Chapters 7 through 9 provide suggestions, not guidance, and surely nothing definitive on how to avoid derailments for presidential candidates, boards, search committees, search firms, and legislators and governors who become involved in the recruitment, selection, and leadership transitions of new presidents. Chapter 7 explores critical elements of the search and selection process, while chapter 8 delves into issues related to board practices and performance. Chapter 9 offers concluding reflections on some of the realities that complicate academic presidencies.

What's in a name? For consistency, we have chosen to use the term "president" to refer to the chief executive officer of the college, university, or system. Chancellor works just as well. Likewise, we use "board members" to refer to the members of the governing body, who at some institutions or systems may be regents or trustees.

Throughout this book, the suggestions we offer are not dispositive—following them assiduously won't prevent every derailment, though precluding a few wouldn't be a bad outcome. Consider our suggestions for what they are: We offer them with respect for the complexities, in all humility, and with no guarantee of success.

Governing boards of academic institutions are composed of dedicated volunteers who contribute their wisdom, time, and personal resources to a noble pursuit—education. While most boards work effectively to find and partner with the president, some have hit bumps in the road. *Presidencies Derailed* identifies some of these bumps and offers suggestions for smoother navigation. Board members are refreshingly human. We all err. As academics, we must also believe that we can all learn how to reduce the chance for error. But human beings are endlessly imaginative and will no doubt continue to find new, innovative ways to mess up and also to do well and good.

Acknowledgments

This book is dedicated to our spouses, Francine Zorn Trachtenberg, Susan Bradshaw, and Linda Bogue, who provided both inspiration and perspective as our work progressed.

We are delighted to acknowledge the assistance provided by several colleagues and friends to the material in this book: Rebecca Hinze-Pifer, Marla Bobowick, Mary Spangler, Paul Martin Wolfe, Sarah Hatoum Hijaz, Greg Britton, Michele Callaghan, and Dana Hecht. Any faults remaining after their diligence are our own.

American higher education is blessed with many excellent presidents whose joys and burdens are known only by their peers and families; they establish and maintain a high standard of excellence and selflessness. Our public and private colleges and universities are the national treasures we celebrate because of the governance of dedicated men and women who volunteer their time, wisdom, and treasure in service as trustees.

Presidencies Derailed

Chapter One

Themes of Presidential Derailment

What is a derailed presidency? Simply stated, a derailment occurs when a president is terminated or forced to resign prior to the end of the term of the first contract—an involuntary departure. Presidential departures, of course, may occur in subsequent contracts and for reasons like those frequently given for derailments. However, when a new president—full of initial promise and public relations fanfare—begins to take his or her institution in harm's way, the institution and the individual can experience unexpected difficult circumstances.

Executive leaders make a difference in organizations. That difference can be positive or negative. A president's understanding of the nature and complexity of the academic enterprise, ethical and moral disposition, interpersonal skill, and political savvy underlie his or her performance and, in turn, the institution's performance. An examination of presidential derailments, inevitably, focuses on the negative impact of ineffective leaders. In the chaos of a derailment, the loss of organizational progress, waste of financial and human resources, and damage to the morale and reputation of those caught in the debris are not fully accounted for in a quantitative analysis but are nonetheless real and sizable.

This makes selecting—and, when necessary, removing—a president the governing board's preeminent responsibility. On this point, it is worth noting that one can see some derailments as evidence that the governance process is working. When early warning signals present themselves, some alert boards have moved to minimize continuing and perhaps more damaging outcomes of an ineffective president or wayward behavior on the part of some board members and civic and political stakeholders who may be contributing to a potential derailment.

The Splendid Complexity of Leadership Effectiveness

Efficiency is doing things right; effectiveness is doing the right things.
PETER F. DRUCKER, *The Effective Executive*

Narratives on presidential derailment are studies in ineffectiveness and are sad and disappointing tales for the individuals and institutions involved. Understanding leadership failures requires exploring its opposite: leadership effectiveness. More than forty years ago in *The Effective Executive*, Peter Drucker suggested that there is no personality syndrome characteristic of the effective executive. Some are shy and others are extroverts, some fat and some lean, some drinkers and some abstainers, some with great interpersonal warmth and some with the coldness of a frozen mackerel. So, what do we know at the end of the day about attributes of effective leaders? Table 1.1 captures a journey through the research and literature in ten main attributes. At its core, leadership boils down to organizational results, collective effort, and individual character.

Leaders in higher education have an added and important requirement: They must understand the nature of the academic enterprise. A college or university must be business-like in many of its functions, but it is not a business. Its missions are complex and sometimes conflicting—educating students to both revere and challenge their cultural heritage and to sometimes reach past the limits of common sense in the search for truth. Its governance processes are built on a lively mix of consensual, political, and bureaucratic principles. Its outcomes and production expectations are complicated and far reaching, embracing multiple outcomes in learning, research, and service. Institutions of higher education are ventures in fact and faith, and most outcomes will not yield to single data point performance evidence (unless *U.S. News and World Report* rankings and ratings are considered a proxy of profit). The early history of American higher education was marked by a desire to keep the devil at bay, and the creation of the colonial college was not a cost-benefit decision. Today's colleges and universities are most assuredly instru-

Table 1.1.   Attributes of effective leaders

1. Facilitate mission clarity and goal achievement
2. Exemplify integrity and credibility
3. Model interpersonal intelligence and build constructive relationships
4. Demonstrate an appreciation for the heritage and culture of the enterprise
5. Exhibit oral and written communication skill
6. Adapt authority and decision style to issue, person, and place—a judicious blend of "tell and compel" with "inquire and inspire"
7. Reflect political wisdom in the capacity to be personal and to discern patterns and sources of decision influence
8. Challenge conventional wisdom and tradition
9. Place the welfare of others before the welfare of self and make developmental investments in colleagues
10. Display a judicious blend of courage and compassion in relationships and decisions

ments of economic development, but their role as guarantors of liberty and open society—celebrating the freedom to critique and challenge—is also not a mission best measured by a cost-benefit analysis.

Leading an organization that is both cultural curator and cultural critic in our society—an organization of multiple missions and goals, complex governance processes, multiple outcomes (not all yielding to easy measurement), and many stakeholders each with different expectations of purpose and performance—might commend equipping presidents with asbestos suits and body armor to handle fire and arrows launched by friends within and without. Yet, giving leadership to an organization deliberately designed to equip men and women in mind, body, spirit, and integrity for a life with meaning and to serve as an arena for the contesting of ideas and policy is a call of nobility worth any challenges a leader might come across.

Beyond the question of collegiate organizational effectiveness, discerning leadership effectiveness is no simple matter. Facile and generally accepted performance indicators are sometimes based on common sense and other times misleading. Did the enterprise grow? Did the leader enjoy increasing levels of prestige? Was the leader visible in the community? Did the leader enjoy the confidence and trust of major stakeholders such as the board and faculty? The value of these criteria is limited. In difficult financial or political moments, a leader who keeps the organization afloat may be eminently effective. Busyness and visibility may add weight to a resume but reveal personal self-interest and not institutional priorities. A leader may be a genial office holder, well-liked by constituents and a cheerleader in front of the parade but may still be empty in substance and style. In any enterprise—corporate, government, or academic—leadership success is an exercise involving questions of splendid complexity:

- How is effectiveness defined? In organizational outcomes and goal achievements, or in the processes employed by the leader? How is it evaluated and who will do the evaluating?
- What attributes mark the effective leader? What skills, attitudes, and understanding come from deep within an individual? What can be learned, cultivated, and adjusted?
- How do ethics shape leadership effectiveness? Is it possible to separate private actions from the public persona of a president? How do you untangle reality from perception and prejudice?

Leadership Failures: The Other Side of the Effectiveness Coin

On the flip side of the ethics effectiveness continuum are situations where it is difficult to tell whether a leader is unethical, incompetent, or stupid.

JOANNE B. CIULLA, "ETHICS AND LEADERSHIP EFFECTIVENESS"

Derailments can be befuddling. How can an academic leader be so recognized for exemplary behavior over his or her career as to be considered presidential material yet fail to develop the skills of working well with others? How can smart people be so dumb, a question explored by Mortimer Feinberg and John J. Tarrant in their book *Why Smart People Do Dumb Things* (1995). What explains the absence or disappearance of interpersonal intelligence? A growing literature details corporate leadership failures. Table 1.2 identifies a taxonomy of ineffective leaders.

Table 1.2.   Attributes of ineffective leaders

1. Incompetence—Absence of will or skill
2. Rigidity—Stiff, unyielding, inflexible
3. Intemperance—Lack of self control
4. Callousness—Uncaring and unkind
5. Corruption—Self-interest ahead of public interest
6. Insularity—A disregard for health and welfare of followers
7. Evil—Use of pain as instrument of power

Source: Bad Leadership by Barbara Kellerman (2004)

This book offers a qualitative glimpse at the events and factors associated with presidential derailments at institutions of higher education. The accounts of presidential derailments profiled in this book range from demonstrations of disappointing ethical lapses and character flaws to poor search processes and weak boards. Can we spot these unfortunate personality problems before they manifest themselves under the pressures of executive expectations? Can we strengthen governance practices and organizational relationships in a way that supports institutional leaders and organizational transitions? These are matters of integrity, courage, and caring.

The Cost of Presidential Derailments

The behavior of top level executives impacts the organizational bottom line.
CHET ROBIE, DOUGLAS BROWN, AND PAUL BLY, "RELATIONSHIP BETWEEN
MAJOR PERSONALITY TRAITS AND MANAGERIAL PERFORMANCE"

Presidents who have been successful for many years, like Lois B. DeFleur at the State University of New York at Binghamton or Graham Spanier at Penn State, can be forced to step down. Presidents who, year after year, received votes of no confidence from faculty senates can remain on the rails, as did John Silber at Boston University. But early derailments are a special case and occur with depressing frequency. How frequent is derailment? Too frequent. Of the fifty college presidents whose careers were derailed in 2009 and 2010, thirty-two had been at public institutions, sixteen at independent institutions, and one at a proprietary institution.

Too many presidents fail to complete the first term of their contract. For the individual institution, it takes only one derailment to impose costs that can never be recouped. For higher education, each derailment erodes public understanding and support which, in turn, undermines institutional autonomy. Why? Many of these presidential derailments could have been prevented. For those who support colleges and universities, derailments reflect bad investments.

The sad narrative of collegiate derailment continues. As we bring this work to press, one reads about the removal of Richard Lariviere at the University of Oregon, and Dan Fogel at the University of Vermont and the removal and subsequent indictment of Graham Spanier at Pennsylvania State University. These are in addition to the "School for Scandal" exits cited in the preface. Dysfunctional presidential performance and president-board relations are regrettably front page news in both the professional and public press. Each detracts from the reputation of higher education at large.

The costs of presidential failure can also be counted in dollars, which may not be the most important currency but are still very real. Dismissal costs are likely to include legal fees and often severance pay. In addition, the institution must find ways to pay the costs of a new search and hiring a new president—not just a new salary, bonuses, and relocation allowances but also salary supplements for interim presidents, legal fees to support contract negotiations, and communications campaigns to manage the message. New presidents often entail housing renovations, office space adjustments, and new furniture and equipment. These expenses take money away from academic priorities.

Other, less quantifiable costs also figure into the equation. Depressed morale and uncertainty among the institution's student body, parents, faculty, staff, board members, alumni, and donors may impact enrollment, retention, fundraising, and institutional loyalty. Some constituents will be overjoyed at the removal of a president perceived to have failed at important parts of the job. Others will be downcast—even the worst presidents had supporters. People hired by the former president will worry about job security, and the best may seek new opportunities elsewhere. Others will jockey for position, hoping for favored treatment in a new administration.

Institutional progress may be stalled in the wake of a derailment. While interim presidents may not be afraid to act, their ability to do so may be constrained by the board or their own trepidation about taking an action that may be overturned by a new president. Tactical rather than strategic planning may rule. If the interim president wishes to become a candidate for the permanent job, she or he may act with an excess of caution in order not to offend any particular constituency.

Often, if the derailment was caused by malfeasance, institutions will create new policies and procedures that are expensive to administer and are generally successful at locking the barn door after the horse has run away. Major donors, foundations, and other grant-making agencies, as well as banks and bond-rating companies, may look askance or hold decisions in abeyance until permanent leadership is in place.

The board has the final say in hiring and firing a president, so it may be the most demoralized about a derailment. The board will take the brunt of criticism from other constituencies and, in turn, will have to guard against recrimination. Because few boards are initially unanimous during either the hiring or the firing, ancient grievances and divisions may awaken. Board members who supported the former president may find themselves considering resignation or fending off attempts to force them off the board.

In addition, the board's workload will increase during the search process. Some board members will urge that haste is essential for institutional stability. Others will counsel a slow pace in the belief that it will ensure success. Especially after a derailment, the board's skittishness about making decisions will likely increase. The temptation and specter of micromanagement will loom in the absence of a chief executive officer.

Causes of Derailment

College, university, and system presidents fail—and succeed—regardless of whether they have held a presidency before; whether they hold doctoral degrees; whether they came from faculty positions or administrative positions or both; whether the bulk of their experience was in industry or government; and whether they have worked in large universities or small colleges, in public or independent institutions, in stand-alone institutions or in statewide systems, in well-endowed or tuition-dependent institutions; in residential or nonresidential campuses, in urban or rural locations, in schools that rely primarily on face-to-face instruction or those that are predominantly online, in secular or religiously affiliated institutions, and in nonprofit or proprietary institutions.

Derailment has a small number of causes and a large number of effects. Three underlying and often overlapping factors can undo a presidency:

1. *Personal shortcomings.* Especially in hindsight, individual failings rise to the top as a major factor in presidential derailments. Some shortcomings are more egregious than others. Unethical behavior must be addressed when discovered. Stubbornness is one challenge, but an individual's inability to adapt to the demands of the presidency is more complicated, not only to diagnose but also to rectify. Poor interpersonal skills and ineffective communication styles are inherently problematic in a college or university's highest office.

2. *Institutional context.* Institutional context centers on the behavior of the president and also on the possibility of deep-seated institutional complexities. First, derailed presidents can demonstrate weaknesses in reading the

organizational culture. Every college, university, and state system is part of the larger field of higher education and an organizational entity with a unique set of circumstances. Appreciating, adjusting to, and accommodating those idiosyncrasies is a prerequisite for success. Some presidents fail to understand or respect the institution's culture and traditions. Some bump into major road blocks from key constituencies, often the board or faculty. Some have problems building and managing a strong leadership team. Second, presidents of talent and integrity can occasionally encounter internal complexities to challenge any collegiate Solomon—fractured and warring faculty, animosities between faculty and administration, encrusted cultures resistant to change and responsiveness, town and gown conflicts, below-the-table political meddling for public institutions or guerrilla action in private institutions from religious partisans unhappy with doctrinal positions of some faculty, and impossible financial or revenue issues. While this book will engage primarily behaviors assigned to presidents and occasionally to boards, these additional internal complications are not to be ignored.

3. *Board shortcomings.* In some derailments, the board is as much a part of the problem as the president. Leadership of academic institutions depends on good governance and a productive board-president relationship. Some presidents fall victim to flawed search processes. Others discover preexisting conditions of board dysfunction, such as micromanagement, weak oversight, or internal schisms. A few stumble into unethical and disheartening board behavior, such as breaches of confidentiality and conflicts of interest.

Research on corporate derailments points to four enduring themes: failure to meet business objectives, problems with interpersonal relationships, inability to lead key constituents, and difficulty adapting (see table 1.3). Although these themes are not meant to be all encompassing, they do represent the most thorough classification of factors associated with derailment in the for-profit business sector. Alas, they are also endemic in institutions of higher education.

When these four themes were used to examine college and university president derailments, two additional themes surfaced: ethical lapses and board shortcomings. The ethical lapses distinguish between other personality factors and inappropriate behavior that were the unfortunate undoing of several presidents. At institutions of higher education, governing boards are an inherent part of the organizational structure and are not without fault in many presidential derailments. The case studies in chapters 2 through 5 re-

Table 1.3.   Enduring derailment themes from the corporate sector

Theme	Characteristics
Failure to meet business objectives	• Poor performance • Lack of follow through • Lack of disciplined judgment • Difficulty thinking strategically or making strategic decisions • Betrayal of trust
Problems with interpersonal relationships	• Insensitivity to others; cold, aloof, arrogant • Overly emotional and mercurial temperament • Isolation from the organization, not open or responsive to honest dissent • Extreme ambition • Authoritarianism • Lack of self-awareness about leadership strengths and weaknesses
Inability to lead key constituents	• Inability to lead a large-scale organization • Failure to staff effectively • Failure to delegate responsibilities • Inability to manage subordinates and develop staff • Overreliance on a single mentor or advisor • Difficulty building and leading a team
Difficulty adapting	• Difficulty adapting to a different culture • Limited capacity to develop or grow professionally • An early strength becomes a weakness • A previous deficiency becomes a liability • Conflict with upper management

Sources: McCall and Lombardo (1983), Morrison et al. (1987), Lombardo and McCauley (1988), Leslie and Van Velsor (1996), Bentz (1985), Gentry et al. (2007)

veal evidence of these six derailment themes and their impact on leadership failures in higher education institutions:

1. Ethical lapses
2. Poor interpersonal skills
3. Inability to lead key constituencies
4. Difficulty adapting
5. Failure to meet business objectives
6. Board shortcomings

Derailment Theme 1: Ethical Lapses

Leadership is a matter of how to be, not how to do it.

Frances Hesselbein, *Hesselbein on Leadership*

The morning press carries frequent headlines about soul erosion in executive suites—of corporate officers embezzling from their companies, of elected politicians engaged in sexual escapades, of nonprofit executives hiring friends and family at above market rates. Sadly, higher education leaders—presidents and board members—are not inoculated against unethical behavior. Personal shortcomings and lapses of judgment can derail a president. Consider these examples of presidential insensitivity, which, as Ciulla noted, may reside only a short distance from executive stupidity.

- What can be said of Althea Collins, president of Bennett College, who expressed surprise when she was criticized for hiring her husband and her daughter in well-paying and highly visible leadership roles? (Foreman, 2002)
- How may we understand the president of the University of Illinois Joseph White and Urbana Chancellor Richard Herman sanctioning an informal admissions process where a "clout" list of applicants received special consideration because of links to trustees, donors, or political officials? (Masterson, 2009)
- How can we explain the University of California Santa Cruz Chancellor Denice Denton moving into the chancellor's residence and spending $30,000 of public dollars to build a dog run? (Fain, 2006)

Character deficits of leaders are costly in many ways. First, when wayward leaders embezzle human and financial resources, they divert resources from legitimate to self-serving uses and diminish the promise of those whose welfare they held in trust. Once a wrongful act is discovered, a second unhappy cost is incurred. Excuses, damage control, and sometimes legal proceedings distract the leader from his or her appointed function and cost money that would otherwise be used for productive purposes.

Other less quantifiable but more pernicious fallouts include a perception of dumbing down decency and a loss of civic and professional trust. The latter is a particularly damaging outcome in a nonprofit enterprise. A loss of trust can produce a loss of participation (including in charitable giving), a potentially fatal outcome for the civic contract between the institution, the people it serves, and the people who support it.

Of the sixteen derailed presidents profiled in the next few chapters, three tripped on ethical standards. While not the most prevalent problem among the derailed presidents, ethical lapses and immoral behavior must be dealt with swiftly and fairly. That burden almost always falls on the board, whose primary concern must be the greater good of the institution.

DERAILMENT THEME 2: POOR INTERPERSONAL SKILLS

Good leaders must first become good servants.
ROBERT K. GREENLEAF, *Servant-Leadership*

In *Good to Great* (2002), Jim Collins isolated two notable attributes of executive leaders who guided their corporations from good to great: a strong sense of self and personal humility, and disciplined commitment and perseverance. When leaders demonstrate the antithesis of this behavior—arrogance, inconsistency, and favoritism—they place their institutions and people in harm's way. In table 1.4, Donald Walker, a former college president, contrasts the attitudes and approaches of effective and ineffective leaders.

College and university presidents interact with a wide range of people—young and old, near and far, rich and poor, traditional and progressive, entitled and disempowered, supportive and resistant. The president has to play well with all of them, even as he or she has responsibility for making difficult

Table 1.4.   Leadership attitudes and approaches

Less effective leaders	More effective leaders
Are much taken with the status, insignia, and privilege of position	Wear the privilege and status of office lightly
Perceive their responsibility as making hard and unpopular decisions	Are good politicians who understand the complexity and interaction of events
	Have self-confidence that enables them to absorb the uncertainty and hostility of others
See the university in a state of pathology requiring their heroic intervention	Are not likely to have bulky egos
	Do not react to dissent as threats to the crown
Believe it is their obligation to resist tendencies to laziness, inertness, and mischief	See themselves as working with faculty and staff colleagues deserving respect and transparency

Source: Adapted from Walker (1979)

and sometimes unpopular decisions. How the president makes the decisions, conveys the messages, and responds to reactions can be as important as the decisions themselves.

Many of the derailed presidents in our case studies had poor interpersonal skills. Some were aloof and egotistical, others were stubborn and intimidating. A few were combative, and several had bad tempers. Often, but not always, poor interpersonal skills went hand in hand with an inability to build lead key constituencies, which is the next derailment theme.

Derailment Theme 3: Inability to Lead Key Constituencies

Effectiveness comes about through enabling others to reach their potential.
Max Depree, *Leadership Is an Art*

The literature on corporate derailments cites the inability to build and lead a team as a common denominator for executive failures. In the context of higher education, presidents have a multitude of teams, or constituent groups, with which they work that include the board, faculty senate, unions, alumni associations, legislatures, among others. The ability to develop collaborative, constructive working relationships with a wide range of stakeholders—board members, faculty, staff, alumni, students, donors, the community, and political leaders—is essential.

This diversity of stakeholders creates a distinct challenge for college, university, and system presidents, especially because the stakeholders often have different and sometimes conflicting interests with each other. The board may demand a balanced budget, and the faculty wants to protect the tenure system. Alumni may be enthusiastic about the athletics department, and major donors are focused on academic scholarships. Presidents can readily find themselves in a setting where the probability of success approaches zero. A governor, a powerful religious leader, or an influential board member may have formed an opinion based on personal preferences, prejudices, or perceptions rather than facts, needs, and performance. Sometimes, an able and adept president may be able to win over detractors. In other cases, he or she may leave the institution, the community, or even the field of higher education.

Almost half of the derailed presidents also fumbled in building and leading a strong, cohesive cabinet of senior staff to support their administration; some seemed to foster schisms in their senior team, others hired individuals without the right expertise for an academic institution. The case studies also suggest that the derailed presidents had particular difficulty developing constructive working relationships with faculty, with governors and other political leaders, and with the board.

Derailment Theme 4: Difficulty Adapting

> Traits conducive to change leadership must be added to the mix, including strategic adaptability, emotional resilience, optimism in the face of bad news, and the ability to work with a board and the academic community to recognize and adapt to change.
>
> Terrence MacTaggart, *Leading Change: How Boards and Presidents Build Exceptional Academic Institutions*

What role does sector, type of organization, time, or context play in leadership success? Might an effective CEO of an automobile company make a good mayor, and vice versa? Former generals have served in university presidencies both successfully and unsuccessfully. Small private college presidents have effectively served public research universities, and vice versa. Does history make leaders, or do leaders make history? A university president with decades of experience went on to serve as a successful corporate executive. A highly successful corporate executive failed miserably as a business school dean.

Effective leaders do not yield the authenticity of their own journey and personality to conformist ideas or formulaic practices. They must first know themselves, and then they must be adept at understanding the world around them. All leaders must read the script for any play in which they plan to perform. Some leaders can make the cultural and mission transfer among different organizations, and some cannot. Academic presidents, and those choosing them, will want to have reasonable belief that an individual has knowledge of the enterprise, professional experience, and individual values closely allied with the culture and expectations of the organization he or she hopes to lead.

New presidencies require adjustment. Presidents with previous presidential experience are the minority. Only 28 percent of presidents have served in that capacity at another institution. And a new president is often new to the institution, with 64 percent of presidents stepping into the chief executive position from another institution (American Council on Education, 2007). Many of the derailed presidents profiled had difficulty adjusting to their new institution's culture and community. Some were out of sync with the community values (e.g., too progressive, too conservative), others were not attuned to preexisting power structures (e.g., between the board and the faculty), and still others pushed too hard and too fast for change (e.g., restructuring). The derailed presidents who followed a beloved predecessor often encountered additional challenges as they questioned past practices and introduced new ideas to the institution.

A new presidency represents change, not just for the individual but also for the institution. (See table 1.5 for a list of behaviors that can help a president lead institutional change.) A new president stands, often alone, on stage in the spotlight. The audience—faculty, cabinet, and board members—should not be passive observers. The new president needs active support from the board, the campus, and the broader community to help facilitate a smooth executive transition.

Table 1.5.   Traits affecting presidents' ability to adapt to change

More functional traits	Less functional traits
Open-mindedness in learning the institution's needs for change and the board's perceptions	Reliance on solutions that have worked elsewhere instead of creative solutions that fit the current situation
Skill in articulating a vision or strategic direction that recognizes the institution's values and inspires participation by the board and other stakeholders	Tendency to focus on isolated problems rather than address problems in the context of a broad vision for change that the board embraces
Ability to work with boards, faculty and staff, and community members in a participatory change mode	Preference for being the sole author of the best ideas when it comes to leading change
Capacity to express sincere respect for others engaged in the dialogue surrounding change, whether in support of or in opposition to it	A strong-minded personality that, while decisive, fails to elicit support or wholehearted participation from board members and others
Strength of character to make decisions, set boundaries, say no to proposals inconsistent with the change plan, and respectfully challenge a board on change issues	Excessive desire to please others and to court the favor of the board or strong-willed members
Personal resiliency and persistence in the face of pushback, criticism, unexpected obstacles, and instances when change does not seem to be progressing as planned	Lack of persistence and difficulty maintaining focus when the pursuit of goals is an uphill struggle

Source: MacTaggart (2011), p. 86

DERAILMENT THEME 5: FAILURE TO MEET ORGANIZATIONAL OBJECTIVES

Effectiveness means you get results.
PETER KOESTENBAUM, *Leadership*

The president may be at the top of the organizational chart, but he or she cannot do it alone. Institutions of higher education are complex, sophisticated enterprises. In the end, however, the president must take ownership of all outcomes, good and bad. Determining if the president is successful is not an easy task. Some goals are easier to identify and measure than others, such as financial ratios, and enrollment and retention rates. Some goals may be driven by the president, such as developing a strategic plan or strengthening relations with the local business community. Others may not be so readily within one person's grasp, such as graduation rates and capital campaign success. Some goals take longer than others to accomplish, such as repairing faculty relations or reviewing the curriculum.

Only a few of the derailed presidents in our case studies failed to meet specific organizational objectives. One ran up a sizeable deficit, another incurred considerable budget overruns, and a third fell short of fundraising goals. That said, shortcomings in this area are cause for concern. The board, in particular, must pay attention to setting reasonable but stretch goals for the president, and then monitoring progress and supporting appropriate course corrections.

DERAILMENT THEME 6: BOARD SHORTCOMINGS

We shall here evaluate leader effectiveness in terms of group performance on the group's primary assigned task.
FRED FIEDLER, *A Theory of Leadership Effectiveness*

Derailments can flow from unfortunate behavior not only on the part of presidents but also by boards. What leads the board to believe it can short-circuit participation in the search process by campus stakeholders? How can board members expect a president to lead the institution with integrity when they themselves have conflicts of interest? Why do boards hire capable presidents and then meddle in internal management matters?

Boards may also be complicit in presidential derailments. As revealed in the case studies that follow, the problems sometimes started during the search, when board members manipulated the process to get the presidential result they desired. Some boards had their own dysfunctional dynamics, including tight inner circles or deep schisms among trustees. Some boards were undermined by conflicts of interest, and others meddled in administrative decisions. Few of the boards involved in the derailments examined in this book fulfilled the responsibilities outlined in table 1.6 using standards of good governance.

Leadership Legacies

The effectiveness of leaders must be judged not by their press clippings but by actual social change measured by intent and by the satisfaction of human needs and expectations.

JAMES MACGREGOR BURNS, *Leadership*

Every president enters the office on day one with at least two theories guiding his or her behavior: a theory of role (What am I supposed to do?) and a theory of effectiveness (How will I judge my performance?). Whether these two theories reside in full mental awareness or at subliminal levels, they surely guide leaders in how they approach the position, how they respond to the institutional climate and social realities in which they work, and how they interact with their colleagues and constituents. A theory of effectiveness

Table 1.6.   Responsibilities of the governing board

1. Ensuring that the institution's mission is current
2. Selecting a chief executive to lead the institution
3. Supporting and periodically assessing the performance of the chief executive and establishing and reviewing the chief executive's compensation
4. Charging the chief executive with the task of leading a strategic planning process, participating in that process, approving the strategic plan, and monitoring its progress
5. Ensuring the institution's fiscal integrity, preserving and protecting its assets for posterity, and engaging in fundraising and philanthropy
6. Ensuring the educational quality of the institution
7. Preserving and protecting institutional autonomy and academic freedom
8. Ensuring that institutional policies and processes are current and properly implemented
9. In concert with senior administration, engaging regularly with the institution's major constituencies
10. Conducting the board's business in an exemplary fashion and with appropriate transparency; ensuring the currency of board governance policies and practices; and periodically assessing the performance of the board, its committees, and its members

Source: Adapted from the Association of Governing Boards (2009)

embraces a theory of legacy—what the leader's journey will bequeath to the institution and those whose labor and devotion give it life.

Presidential legacies turn not only on the individual's theories of role and effectiveness but also on their actions and interactions. All leaders—college, university, and system presidents among them—also leave with a legacy. Former University of California President Kerr noted that he left office the same way he entered: "fired with enthusiasm." This double entendre referred, of course, to an enthusiastic entry into office and an enthusiastic firing engineered by then Governor Ronald Reagan.

The media coverage carrying the appointment of a new president is likely to be marked with a celebratory flavor, a herald of optimistic tone, a biographical sketch detailing a glowing past that presumably equips the new president for coming salutary performance, and the pomp and circumstance of an inauguration. Unfortunately, some college and university presidents who entered with wide acclaim of their promise, who orchestrated richly appointed inaugurals, and who, with brief tenure, surrendered the presidential medallion exited with shameful and sad endings very much at odds with the glowing beginning.

Fortunately, most presidents leave behind a more constructive legacy—worthy and noble goals achieved in concert with able colleagues, academic institutions of enriched promise and potential, faculty and staff of enhanced skill, perhaps the grudging respect of those with whom they have contended and disagreed, and cultures that inspire curiosity, courage, and compassion.

"You're fired! Read all about it!"

PART I / Presidents Off-Track

Presidential Derailments at Private Liberal Arts Institutions

Jason McNeal

The Nature of Private Liberal Arts Colleges

The private liberal arts higher education tradition within the United States can trace its roots to the medieval European university, which in turn had its roots in classical Greece and Rome. The seven liberal arts of antiquity (grammar, rhetoric, logic, geometry, arithmetic, music, and astronomy) evolved into the current model as the higher education landscape within the United States diversified.

Today, private liberal arts colleges in this country can be characterized generally as providing a primarily residential, teaching-focused student experience. While online learning does occur in this setting, it is not the principal vehicle of instruction. In addition, while some private liberal arts institutions provide professional or even vocational training, the bulk of these institutions remain focused on educating students through exposure to a broad portfolio of academic disciplines. The aim of a liberal arts experience is to develop general intellectual capabilities and cultivate a love of learning that will last a lifetime.

Many private liberal arts institutions educate three thousand or fewer students each year and have low student-to-faculty ratios. Most were established decades or centuries ago as communities for intellectual, spiritual, and physical development. Many of the institutions are located beyond the beaten path of interstate highways, and such close-knit, communal environments foster unusually strong lifelong relationships with and among students (as evidenced by impressive alumni giving percentages, sometimes above 30 percent). However, in today's world, these remote environments and their lack of "just-in-time" online learning options are often seen as barriers for future growth of liberal arts institutions.

Since most liberal arts institutions operate as private and distinct 501(c) (3) organizations, governing board composition and practices are private, or independent, as well. The governing boards of private liberal arts colleges typically range in size from fifteen to forty members. Boards of private liberal arts institutions are usually self-perpetuating and especially focused on generating income through private philanthropy. Institutions typically seek alumni, community leaders, business executives, and others to serve as board members. While many boards of religiously affiliated liberal arts colleges have seats reserved for clergy or other church-nominated members, the characteristics of affluence and influence are most typical and most valued for the bulk of the members.

Derailment Themes

This chapter examines four discrete presidential derailments at private, liberal arts colleges (see table 2.1). These case studies are based on confidential interviews with participants with firsthand knowledge of the derailment, and their names and institutional details have been disguised to maintain their anonymity. The institutions ranged in student populations from a thou-

Table 2.1.   Profile of private liberal arts college case studies

Characteristic	Institution			
	Caroline College	Seaside College	Medial College	Beneficial College
Student enrollment	2,200	1,000	3,000	3,000
Student-to-faculty ratio	13:1	18:1	15:1	12:1
Endowment (in millions)	$100	$20	$100	$300
Percent of student who live on campus	70	50	75	90
Faith-based character	Historic but not active	Historic but not active	Active	Active

sand to three thousand and had endowments between $20 million and $300 million.

Five derailment themes were identified in the four cases, as shown in table 2.2. The first four themes relate to the behaviors, skills, and abilities of the derailed president. The fifth theme involves board dysfunction, both in performance and in ethical lapses. This theme highlights contextual and systemic factors which can be difficult, if not improbable, for a new president to change or otherwise impact directly.

DERAILMENT THEME: FAILURE TO MEET BUSINESS OBJECTIVES

In recent years, crafting and successfully implementing strategic and financial plans have taken on increased importance for academic institutions. Not only does thoughtful planning provide an institution with a broad vision, goals, and objectives, it also details how the institution aims to fund its ambitions. Increasingly, outside credit rating agencies, such as Moody's investors services and Standard & Poor's Financial Services, analyze an institution's leadership and ability to meet key strategic and financial objectives when assessing credit worthiness.

For private colleges that receive no direct governmental financial assistance based on enrollment figures, a culture of effective planning has contributed to sustained institutional progress. While the governing board has responsibility for approving strategic and financial plans, the president is charged with implementing those plans and goals. For a president of a private institution, few goals matter more than student enrollment, fundraising

Table 2.2.   Derailment themes at private liberal arts colleges

Theme	President			
	Samuel at Seaside College	Carol at Caroline College	Michael at Medial College	Ben at Beneficial College
1. Failure to meet business objectives	X	X		
2. Inability to lead key constituencies		X	X	
3. Poor interpersonal skills	X			X
4. Difficulty adapting				X
5. Board shortcomings		X	X	

revenue, and budget benchmarks. Two derailment case studies illustrate what happens when a president fails to meet institutional goals.

CASE STUDY: *Seaside College*

Seaside College is a regional institution with strong pre-professional programs in business, education, and the sciences. The science program is a particular strength, with many students going on to medical school or other related graduate programs. Seaside serves approximately one thousand undergraduate students, has a $20 million endowment, and is religiously affiliated. Located in a rural setting, it is highly residential and all first-year students are required to live on campus.

Samuel, the derailed president, came to Seaside after serving as president of another private liberal arts college. He had a reputation as a smart academic leader with a big smile and a history of increasing enrollment numbers at two previous institutions. Intent on increasing tuition revenue through enrollment management, the board of Seaside saw Samuel as an ideal match for its institutional goals.

Under Samuel's leadership, enrollment increased, as did the size of the faculty and administration. At the same time, the tuition discount rate rose and retention rates plummeted, creating a substantial annual financial shortfall for this tuition-dependent, private institution. Exacerbating the problem, Samuel was not transparent with financial information and had a hot temper. The combination was not good for his presidency or the institution. During the final year of Samuel's presidency, Seaside faced a $750,000 budget deficit.

Apparently, Samuel did not see the complete financial picture. He focused on enrollment numbers to the exclusion of other related and important factors. As a vice president noted, "He did grow enrollment, but he only cared about the incoming class number. Retention was terrible, and we were discounting tuition far too much."

Likewise, the board questioned the financial model. As one board member explained: "We had an enrollment goal that we thought would be good because the physical plant of the campus could hold more students." Samuel repeatedly assured the board that each additional student added revenue to the bottom line. Yet, when the institution was at full capacity, Seaside was losing money.

Samuel increased Seaside's employment costs before the revenue stream could support it. He expanded the size of the faculty and the administration and increased salaries, assuming that these additional expenses would be covered by increased donations. The latter was particularly problematic given the way Samuel managed the development function. He did not have a fundraising background, nor did he get personally involved in it. Instead, he outsourced the development function by hiring two consultants who lived more than 100 miles from the close-knit Seaside community. As one board member noted, "He left that function of the college unattended for two years."

At Seaside College, Samuel also had a "hot temper that got in the way of everything," as one board member noted. Samuel's problems with interpersonal relationships were compounded by a lack of communication. He did not fully disclose important information about the college to his cabinet (information they needed to manage the enterprise) or the board (information they needed to govern the enterprise). One vice president noted that "he was cliquish with his administrative team. You knew very quickly if you were inside or not. He was unforgiving if you weren't on his side." Another vice president found his meetings with the president cancelled for months in the wake of a public comment about the college's poor financial situation.

Samuel's lack of transparency with the board verged on the unethical. A member of his administrative team said that Samuel "sugar-coated . . . or withheld reports and information from the board, faculty, and his cabinet." For example, he waited four months before sharing with the board an accreditation report that required the institution to make progress on key financial issues.

As a board member observed, "The secrecy went all the way through the school. Vice presidents couldn't communicate with the board. The president wasn't communicating with the vice presidents. The vice presidents, when they did communicate with him, were ignored or even worse. . . . He told some of his vice presidents not to share any information with their subordinates or anyone else. So he really clamped down on things." Ultimately, this attempt to control information and, in turn, buy time, backfired. Unable to hide the $750,000 deficit, Samuel eventually was forced to resign.

CASE STUDY: *Caroline College*

Carol at Caroline College also failed to meet operational goals, but for different reasons. Caroline College educates approximately 2,200 students.

It has a regional reputation as a rigorous academic institution with a strong nationally recognized athletic program. It is church-related, with an endowment of more than $100 million, and a student-to-faculty ratio of 13:1. The institution is highly residential, with more than 70 percent of students choosing to live on its single campus.

Carol, the derailed president, came to Caroline College as the sitting and, by all accounts, effective president of another faith-based, private liberal arts college. At Caroline College, Carol followed a very successful and beloved president. During the fifteen-year tenure of the former president, the institution had doubled its enrollment from a thousand to two thousand, expanded its facilities with several new buildings, and achieved ambitious fundraising goals. In short, Caroline College had a strong sense of forward momentum.

Carol was strongly committed to the college's religious roots, much more so than the student body and surrounding community. In fact, a clash of values and culture may have played an important role in Carol's firing. She did not socialize much, which may have alienated some influential board members. When she tried to bring best practices into the boardroom, she was met with resistance. A capital campaign that began under her tenure stalled. When Caroline College's positive momentum reached a plateau and then began to decline, the board held Carol responsible.

At Caroline College, it soon became apparent that institutional financial, enrollment, budgeting, and fundraising goals were barely being met. A consultant who worked closely with Carol during her tenure observed, "The biggest change that I saw was that the school had lost its momentum. They had begun a capital campaign under the new president, and it wasn't going anywhere. The growth in enrollment that they had experienced the previous decade had hit a plateau and had started to decline."

Most of the benchmarks in enrollment and fundraising were met by Carol's administration, but only by the slimmest of margins. During the previous fifteen years, the Caroline College's board of the institution had grown accustomed to explosive growth. When that growth slowed considerably, they became noticeably concerned about the new president's capabilities.

Derailment Theme: Inability to Lead Key Constituencies
Academic institutions have multiple constituencies: students, alumni, faculty, staff, board members, government agencies, community leaders. The list

is long and diverse. Given their private (versus public) status and close-knit community feel, liberal arts institutions, especially, engage many constituencies in campus life. Presidents in these settings are wise to recognize the socio-political landscape of their institutions, to understand the power of key constituencies, and to engage, personally, people of influence and affluence. Such efforts provide the president with needed intelligence about the institution and also build social and political capital should it be needed.

The second derailment theme is an inability of the president to form relationships with key constituents. Various individuals may offer the president counsel, friendship, encouragement, or other assistance, and they also may buffer the president from ad hominem criticisms. Without strong support, minor presidential missteps lead more readily to derailments.

In Carol's situation, she did not cultivate strong relationships with key constituents, including faculty, board members, and local community leaders. A vice president described a missed opportunity. On the Wednesday before Thanksgiving, when little work is done on campus, Carol was in her office and her calendar was clear. This vice president suggested she drop in to chat with a few members of the faculty and staff. As he recollected, "She didn't do it. She didn't have to do what I told her, of course. But she just didn't do those little things that could have torn down some walls."

Nor did Carol build strong rapport with board members. One trustee observed, "She had the wherewithal, but she wasn't enough of the 'attend the social events, go to the country club, golf, sit down, and have a drink' kind of president. I think she could have done it, but she didn't see that as a presidential role."

Carol viewed her role as president in a more formal way. Neither she nor her husband consumed alcohol, and alcohol was not permitted on campus. So, Carol decided that it was not wise for her to hold events in the president's home that included alcohol, and she opted out of many social settings where alcohol would be served. Her decisions around alcohol and her lack of attendance at less official, more social gatherings (like casual country club events), encouraged some board members to view her as a stick-in-the-mud and even haughty.

It appeared that Carol's difficulty in leading key campus constituencies was rooted in her personal beliefs and religious practices. The bulk of the student body and the surrounding community were of a different religious tradition than the college's historical church connection. Carol shared the same faith tradition of the college and invested herself early in religious activities on campus. For example, as a vice president observed, "She openly displayed her interest in religion and her personal Christian life. At her inauguration, at her request, we had a ceremony in our chapel where people laid hands on her. That seemed a little too demonstrative for some of our very conservative folks."

In the end, a small group of influential board members surprised Carol by asking her to leave the presidency. While no single reason was given to Carol for the board's decision and while she remained steadfast in her belief that the request was unjustified, she realized that she did not have the necessary good will from enough of the board to weather the storm. Ultimately, the board suggested that the reason for her derailment was that Caroline College had started to falter under her leadership. While quantitative signs of weakness had started to surface (as mentioned previously), the fact that she did not have needed relational capital contributed to Carol's premature departure. A similar problem arose for Michael at Medial College, but his difficulties were even more closely tied to a shortage of strong personal relationships.

Case Study: *Medial College*

Medial College educates approximately three thousand undergraduate students each year. It is a faith-based institution with a strong music program (and multiple touring music ensembles) and a deep commitment to global education (more than 50 percent of the students study abroad). It is highly residential, with more than 75 percent of students living on campus.

Michael, the derailed president, came to Medial College after having served as a president of a smaller private liberal arts institution. Like Carol, he had the unenviable task of following on the heels of a revered president. His predecessor had graduated from the college, taught as a professor there, served as president for nearly twenty-five years, and still regularly attended campus and alumni events.

The board hired Michael with a mandate for change. As Michael himself explained, "When I was hired, the board told me that they wanted a new direction. The institution wasn't broken, and it didn't need to be fixed in any major way. But, they wanted to take the institution to a new level of excellence. They said they wanted change, but they really didn't want change. I enacted change. And I didn't know that there were problems until I got the phone call from the board chair asking for my resignation."

Under the shadow of a long-standing president, Michael was asked to take Medial College in a different direction, and he publicly thanked his predecessor on numerous occasions. As Michael got to work, a feeling of excitement began to percolate throughout the Medial community. But, when he attempted to make changes in personnel and institutional direction, faculty and staff began to complain directly to the board.

Michael believed he was following the board's guidance and working with key constituencies, but his perception of the strength of his personal relationships was poor. As a consultant working with Medial at the time explained, "He really was blindsided. Some people were complaining about his leadership. But, he didn't have the relationships built strongly enough with the right people to survive." Clearly, he needed productive, strong relationships with the board, administration, and faculty leaders in order to weather some of the more difficult points of transition—both the executive leadership transition and the transformation of the college.

Derailment Theme: Poor Interpersonal Skills

The roles, responsibilities, and expectations of college presidents are broad. Not only does the president serve as the chief executive of an education business, but he or she also oversees several attending businesses: an athletic complex, a hotel, food service, entertainment programs and venues, and facilities management. Some liken the college presidency to the job of city mayor—varied and expansive. To serve successfully in this position, a president must have a clear understanding of and ability to perform these varied functions for a complex enterprise. Equally important, he or she must be able to effectively build and sustain professional and personal relationships. The third derailment theme, poor interpersonal skills, includes such personality traits and relationship styles as an inability to control anger, a dictatorial management style, a harsh and unforgiving demeanor, and a secretive approach to sharing information.

Case Study: *Beneficial College*

Beneficial College is regularly ranked as one of the finest private liberal arts institutions in the country. It has a reputation as a rigorous academic institution with excellent science and music programs and an active study abroad program. Beneficial is strongly related to the church, possesses an endowment of more than $300 million, and a student-to-faculty ratio of 12:1.

Ben, the derailed president, came to Beneficial College after serving as president at a smaller, less prestigious liberal arts institution. When he arrived, campus morale was low. Fewer than half of the faculty reported satisfaction with their work. Ben struck others as an affable and charismatic figure who "made people feel good about being on the team and serving the institution." He was also vocal—and direct—about his positions on sensitive topics. His progressive political views were in keeping with those of the faculty and students, but not necessarily the board or local community.

Despite his general good nature, Ben had a quick temper and sharp tongue. Periodically and unexpectedly, he would have strong but brief outbursts of anger. At least once, he verbally attacked a board member who questioned the wisdom of implementing a major project that the board had previously approved. After that meeting and at the board's suggestion, Ben agreed to work with an executive coach to help him deal more compassionately and effectively with people. Despite progress, the board soon asked for Ben's resignation.

Ben's periodic displays of anger caught people off guard. As one vice president explained, "It was a scary transformation because, generally, he's such a wonderfully friendly, outgoing, and warm guy. It didn't happen very often, but once every couple months something would spark it. It was an unusual manifestation that would only last three or four minutes, and then he would apologize. It didn't sit well with people who happened to bear the brunt of it."

These incidents became increasingly problematic, causing people to question whether Ben was the right leader for the college. In hindsight, Ben himself could point to the confrontation—when he publicly chastised a board member—from which there was no turning back. As he reflected, "I think the board meeting where I got angry was a big event. If I hadn't gotten angry, I would still be there. . . . My angry response was not appropriate, and that was never forgotten."

DERAILMENT THEME: DIFFICULTY ADAPTING

To succeed, a president must be able to operate effectively within the multiple roles of the presidency and the complicated culture of academic institutions. Especially at private, liberal arts colleges, presidents regularly must engage with and manage expectations for disparate constituencies that hold varied perspectives on how best to run the academic enterprise. Alumni, faculty, staff, board members, donors, community leaders, and even the church at times, may have visions for the institution that vary widely or may be polar opposites.

A college president may be called upon to meet with students, craft a multimillion-dollar gift solicitation, participate in a faculty meeting, and manage a board meeting—all in a single day. The inability of a president to move among these different cultures and constituencies is a common cause of derailment.

For example, Ben at Beneficial College did not adapt to the community's more conservative culture. According to one board member, he was much appreciated by faculty and students for his progressive political views: "The faculty liked him a good bit, and that's not easy here. They liked the fact that he was willing to take stands on issues and that he was typically in agreement with their worldview. Whether it was medical rights for homosexual partners or the war in Iraq, he was vocal." However, he was unable to convince other, more conservative constituencies that he was leading the institution in the right direction.

Ben himself explained, with emotion: "I was aggressive for pressing for more diversity on campus. There is nothing wrong with our present students—white and of our denomination—but that group is diminishing. Practically speaking, we were going to need different students. . . . Many older constituents wanted the school to be the same school that they remembered—white, upper middle class, and heterosexual."

Ben did not view this as an inability of his to adapt. Instead, he viewed it as a clash of worldviews. He explained: "To me, it's clear that I was let go because we had a difference in philosophies about life. I was more progressive, and the board was not ready for that. I'm not sure there is much that could have been done. We talked about the need for student diversity in my interview, but I don't believe, in retrospect, that they really wanted that." For college presidents, navigating the line between personal beliefs and community values is not easy. But, it does raise a larger issue: How much should (and how should) a president adjust his or her personal philosophy when it is not in alignment with key institutional constituencies?

DERAILMENT THEME: BOARD SHORTCOMINGS
Board Dysfunction

A president's skills, abilities, or failures are not always solely responsible for his or her derailment. At Caroline College and Medial College, board dysfunction contributed to the presidents' decline. These two boards did not adhere to commonly accepted good governance practices, such as formal presidential performance reviews and effective communications within the board or with the president. These shortcomings were exacerbated by a lack of clarity or consensus about the college's direction.

At Caroline College the executive committee kept their perception of the president's poor performance to itself. In fact, Carol explained, "I had asked for a presidential evaluation each year and received only informal feedback from the executive committee of the board. At one point, the board said they were planning a 360 evaluation, and I was grateful, but it never occurred. Had I known more about the perceived problems, I could have done something earlier."

Nor was the rest of the board informed of Carol's performance problems. When the executive committee did not support renewing Carol's contract, it revealed a fracture in board unity. According to a board member, "There was a division within the board—with some saying, 'Hey, we didn't know it was going so badly.' The executive committee was more on the inside and understood it. There was a two-tiered board in many ways, and that was a flaw." Carol herself expressed considerable regret: "I knew I could get the majority of the board to support me, but I didn't have confidence that the board was strong enough to displace the executive committee members. So I said, 'We're going to leave, we're going to step aside.'"

Medial College had good policies and procedures in place to guide board-president communications, but they were not followed. One of the complicating factors was the powerful presence of the retired president. Michael believed he was hired to take the college in a new direction. When he did, he began to encounter covert resistance. Some leaders on campus and in the community began to complain. A vice president said, "The former president and another board member manipulated the board chair. They decided that the 'change' occurring at the institution was not good, and they worked behind the scenes with the previous president to force Michael out." While such Machiavellian maneuvering may seem implausible, the retired president agreed to serve as interim president immediately following Michael's resignation.

Also troubling was a lapse in Michael's annual performance evaluation. The board had in place well-thought-out policies and procedures for presidential evaluations. In fact, Michael was evaluated every year, except the final year, and had received all "A" ratings. "Apparently," according to a board member, "those evaluations didn't mean anything. . . . The chair of the board affairs committee oversaw the evaluation process, and he was the one given responsibility by the board to develop a very detailed process of evaluation. As the chair, he also had the responsibility to see that this process was followed. He was the one individual who could have and should have 'stopped the train' by insisting on following the process."

When Michael's resignation was requested, no discernible process was followed. Indeed, one board member explained, "Most on the board were stunned. They thought things were going well. We met for five hours, debating whether or not to accept his resignation. In the end, no one would stand up for following a process. But two board members did stand up and resign from the board in the middle of that meeting. It was just weakness on the part of the board."

Ethical Lapses by the Board

Even more insidious than boards that do not follow established procedures are boards—which have ultimate accountability and responsibility for the college—that violate ethical standards. At Caroline College, conflicts of interest were not uncommon. For example, the four board members on the investment committee served as active fund managers for Caroline College, and the institution had no practice of seeking bids through a request for proposals process. A vice president shared his astonishment and dismay: "They were not competitive bidding contracts with vendors! The contracts were going to friends of friends, and most of the friends were connected to the board chair!"

The board chair served as legal counsel for the college, creating another level of conflicts of interest and confusion. With anguish, Carol recalled her concerns about their conversations, "I was never clear about whether I was talking to the board chair or whether I was talking to our legal counsel. Was he giving me advice, as my counsel, that I could accept or reject? Or was he telling me, as board chair, what I was supposed to do?"

Carol quietly attempted to address these conflicts of interest and vendor contracting processes by taking board members to the Association of Governing Board meetings and gently raising these accountability issues. "But," as one participant vice president said, "you have a long-time board member who likes to throw his weight around, and he doesn't want to give it up. So, he starts sowing seeds of doubt about the leadership of the president."

Conclusion

The factors associated with presidential derailments are as varied as the institutions in which they occur. While the experiences of these four private liberal arts colleges may not be generalized to other institutions, common principles can be drawn from them. First, the president and the board can play critical roles in averting derailments. Presidents must possess the capacity to meet institutional goals, build relationships with key constituencies and individuals, manage interpersonal relationships effectively, and be flexible in navigating cultures, traditions, and their own preferences. Boards must understand their roles and carry out their responsibilities with the utmost of integrity and within the parameters of good governance practices.

Second, long-standing, successful, and beloved presidents leave big shoes to fill. Their successors seem to face greater difficulties in navigating an executive transition. Presidents who accept such challenges may benefit from greater clarity about expectations and more frequent communication from the board as they settle into their new role. Similarly, boards should be mindful of these delicate leadership transitions. Under these circumstances, they should be even more conscious of and conscientious about providing the new president with a unified voice on priorities and publicly visible support.

Finally, presidential evaluations should be an ongoing conversation, punctuated by annual or biannual formal reports, which assess and provide feedback to the new president. Not only are evaluations that assess the president's capacity to manage the functions of the enterprise important, but evaluations that assess the president's softer skills and relationship-building capacity appear to be a key in avoiding derailments.

Chapter Three

Presidential Derailments at Public Master's Level Institutions

Julie Longmire

The Nature of Public Master's Level Universities

According to the Carnegie Foundation for the Advancement of Teaching, there are more than 650 public master's level institutions in the United States and its territories. Public master's level institutions are primarily regionally based state universities with a mission to educate people from the surrounding counties. Institutions of this type typically have a strong service orientation and offer an array of majors such as education, nursing, engineering, and the liberal arts. Their primary mission is teaching as opposed to research, and they tend to educate more undergraduates than graduates. Their graduate programs are often based on degrees that bolster local communities, such as a master's in education aimed at providing advanced training for local school teachers.

Presidents at master's level universities come from a variety of backgrounds, but the majority have served as chief academic officer or provost before becoming president for the first time. In 2007, the average tenure for public master's level presidents had risen to 8.1 years from 6.5 years in 1986. Thirty-five percent of presidents at master's colleges and universities had been in their present positions for more than ten years (American Council on Education, 2007). However, not all presidents are long-serving. From 2000 to 2010, more than twenty-nine public master's level presidents had derailed—been fired or asked to resign within the first five years of taking office.

Derailment Themes

This chapter specifically looks at the causes of derailment of four presidents at public master's level institutions (see table 3.1). These case studies are based on confidential interviews with participants who have firsthand knowledge of the derailment, and their names and institutional details have been disguised to maintain their anonymity. The institutions ranged in size from 3,500 students to 19,500 students and employed between 350 and a thousand full-time staff and faculty. Participating institutions were located in both rural and urban communities and were geographically dispersed throughout the United States.

What events led to the derailment of presidents at four master's level public institutions? Each university experienced a distinct set of events, but some commonalities surfaced: disagreements over real estate deals, academic reorganizations, and unpopular hiring decisions of key academic personnel. Four common derailment themes emerged from these case studies (see table 3.2):

1. *Difficulty adapting.* In three of the four cases, the presidents failed to understand, appreciate, and respect the university's culture. They were not able to adjust to a different institutional environment.

2. *Inability to lead key constituencies.* All four presidents had difficulty building, managing, and leading the senior team. Three of the four had contentious relationships with faculty. Two presidents also had ad-

Table 3.1.   Profile of public master's level university case studies

Characteristic	Institution			
	Central Plains State University	Overland State University	Ridge State University	University of South Hogan
Student enrollment	3,500	7,000	19,000	4,500
Student-to-faculty ratio	6:1	14:1	19:1	13:1
Undergraduate-to-graduate ratio (%)	58:42	94:6	78:22	45:55
Governance structure	Institutional board appointed by governor	System board appointed by governor	System board appointed by governor	Institutional board appointed by governor
State system or independent campus	Independent campus	State system	State system	Independent campus

Table 3.2.   Derailment themes at public master's level universities

	President			
Theme	Oscar at Overland State University	Richard at Ridge State University	Charlie at Central Plains State University	Howard at University of South Hogan
1. Difficulty adapting	X	X	X	
2. Inability to lead key constituencies	X	X	X	X
3. Poor interpersonal skills	X	X		X
4. Ethical lapses		X		

versarial relationships with the state, one with the legislature and the other with the statewide system for higher education.

3. *Poor interpersonal skills.* Three of the four derailed presidents had problems developing relationships because they did not communicate effectively.

4. *Ethical lapses.* One of the presidents was derailed because of ethical failures.

DERAILMENT THEME: DIFFICULTY ADAPTING

Each academic institution is unique. Newcomers must understand and appreciate the organizational mission, traditions, and culture. An executive transition requires an adjustment by all, as a new president immerses himself or herself in the university's community and as the campus adapts to a new chief executive. Presidential inability to adapt at these master's level institutions included behaviors that were viewed as demonstrating a lack of belief in the nature and mission of the institution and an unwillingness to understand its culture. Examples included presidents who were unable to change their leadership style to be more collegial, were unwilling to champion the institution's mission, and resisted the authority from the larger university system. This set of failures was observed in Central Plains, Overland, and Ridge State Universities.

CASE STUDY: *Overland State University*

Overland State University is a medium-sized, public master's level university located in a rural community. Primarily an undergraduate institution, Overland offers more than forty undergraduate majors and six graduate degrees. It operates in three satellite locations and leads the state system in online degree programs for nontraditional students. It also has strong partnerships with local high schools to facilitate dual credit programs.

When Oscar arrived, Overland was in the midst of a growth cycle. Undergraduate admissions had increased, and the university was hiring more faculty. Within six months, Oscar had combined different colleges, schools, and departments into a new structure.

Oscar was perceived by many as arrogant and condescending—on and off campus. He hired a provost with a similar attitude, who later denied tenure to several well-respected junior faculty.

Within eighteen months of Oscar's appointment, a well-respected senior faculty member sent a letter to the system chancellor, as well as local and state media outlets, calling for the president's resignation. The letter described how Oscar was damaging campus morale and the university's reputation with community members and alumni. Within days, the chancellor—with support from the board—relieved Oscar of his duties as president and relegated him to an administrative position for the remainder of his contract. At Overland State University, Oscar exuded the attitude of an "anointed one." One participant described Oscar's demeanor as "You guys don't really know what you're doing. But, don't worry, I'm here to save you." His presumption of superiority rubbed folks the wrong way at this rural institution. Overland's campus culture was extremely collegial and included a strong commitment to consensus building. This was not Oscar's modus operandi. Rather than taking time to get to know the community and soliciting input, he usually announced his decisions: "Here's what we are going to do. Now let's do it." For example, almost immediately upon taking office, Oscar engineered an unpopular academic reorganization that was widely viewed as a ploy to shift power away from a strong dean. The new academic structure had not been openly discussed and debated among faculty, deans, and administrators. While he had appointed a task force of faculty members to guide the reorganization, task force members indicated that their role was "merely for show."

CASE STUDY: *Ridge State University*

Ridge State University is a large, public master's level university located in a major metropolitan city. It offers more than a hundred undergraduate majors and master's degree programs. It is part of a large statewide system of master's level institutions, with a central board that is appointed by the governor. The president of Ridge State reports to the state chancellor.

Richard had grand plans for Ridge State, but they were at odds with the needs of a public university that had a mandate to serve the local community. He bristled against the restrictions imposed by the state system and tried to orchestrate a merger with a community college. He also neglected important town-gown relationships.

Richard's credibility was tarnished quickly. In the early months of his presidency, he spearheaded an unpopular faculty retrenchment. Then, when confronted with opposition, he made an about face and said that the plan had not been his idea. Also within his first year, he was named as a finalist for another college presidency. First, he denied it, and then he provided a flimsy explanation.

Finances, however, were Richard's ultimate undoing. Under his leadership, the university exceeded its budget by several million dollars, and the Ridge State University Foundation restricted his access to funds. The proverbial last straw was a funding commitment that never materialized. Eventually, the state system released him from his duties as president. A president with questionable ethics and severely damaged credibility was no longer viable. At Ridge State University, Richard failed to adapt to the culture and traditions of a public university with a responsibility to all students. During a public meeting, which later garnered national media attention, Richard made derogatory comments about underprepared students. Clearly, he did not embrace the mission of Ridge State, which served the local community, many of whom required remedial education. The central university administration viewed the measure of excellence as the "value-added" that graduates attained. Richard also failed to understand and accept the limitations of his role within the system. Wanting autonomy over the university, he tried to merge his campus with a local community college so he could sever ties with the central administration. As one participant observed, "Anyone who would be president in this system has to be very willing to work in a very tight system. Our presidents do not have the flexibility that you would have in lots of other places." Having failed to work within the parameters of the system, Richard found himself in direct conflict with the board of the statewide system.

Derailment Theme: Inability to Lead Key Constituencies

The second major reason for derailment, observed at all four universities, involved the presidents' failure to work with key constituencies including faculty, governing boards, state legislatures, system administration, alumni and other donors, and the local community. In two of the institutions, this was compounded by ineffective leadership teams of loyalists to the president. Communications often contributed to the derailed presidents' inability to build consensus among the key stakeholders of their universities. They rarely sought feedback from faculty, the cabinet, or the board, when making important decisions for the university. For example, Richard at Ridge State University was often described as having grandiose plans for the institution, but he failed to lay the groundwork to obtain support from major constituencies. One participant noted, "He overreached all the time. He wanted headlines. He wanted to be massively successful." But, as another added, "He would just announce what they were going to do, and do it. He didn't get buy-in from people." The presidents at Overland and South Hogan (see the case study below) had similarly poor communication skills that contributed to their inability to lead key constituencies.

Faculty

As chief executive of the institution, a university president needs to have a strong cabinet and productive relations with faculty. None of the four derailed presidents had constructive relationships with the faculty. In some cases, the faculty was predisposed against the president because of reorganizations. In others, the president tried—unsuccessfully—to establish positive working relationships with the faculty.

Case Study: *Central Plains State University*

Central Plains State University is a small, public master's level university located in a rural setting. It offers more than twenty undergraduate majors and nearly a dozen master's degree programs through higher education centers throughout the state, including a distance education program. It is an independent campus, and its board is appointed by the governor.

Higher education was a new field for Charlie, the derailed president, whose prior work experience included law and government. He had an authoritarian approach to leadership and, along the way, antagonized many campus constituents. His relationship with faculty was tenuous at best. He did not understand shared governance, nor was he a proponent of the tenure system. As one participant stated, "He just couldn't wrap his head around it." Charlie made some unpopular recommendations on tenure. Allegations of racial discrimination were voiced by members of the faculty. Ultimately, the American Association of University Professors sanctioned the university, and several faculty members filed lawsuits alleging racial discrimination.

Despite his political connections, Charlie had difficulty working with the state legislature. During his presidency, appropriations from the state legislature declined. He was also dismissive of the board, treating it as a symbolic structure with no real authority. To make matters worse, he surrounded himself with a new slate of vice presidents, many without a strong background in higher education.

Due to his visibility in the community, the board tried hard to find a way to keep Charlie at Central Plains. Many of his campus duties were reassigned to a vice president in the hopes that she could serve as a chief operating officer. The board asked Charlie to focus on external relations and especially fundraising, which was one of his strengths. However, Charlie's personality and leadership style made it difficult for the vice presidents to take action without his approval. In the end, after trying this new structure for six months, the board dismissed Charlie as president.

Charlie's problems with faculty at Central Plains State University stemmed from his inability to work within the shared governance model of academic institutions. For example, Charlie wanted to introduce a new major at Central Plains. As one participant explained, "Those are the kind of things that he would get really excited about. But, the faculty hadn't bought into them. When he would say, 'This is where we're going,' the faculty would sit on the sidelines. . . . He had one view of how to get to a place, and the faculty had a different view."

Charlie's management style went against the participatory ideals of higher education. Campus leaders described him as "very aggressive" and "manipulative." Charlie did not foster open dialogue among various constituencies, nor did he seek input from stakeholders about changes at Central

Plains. He was known to call faculty members into his office and demand that they publicly support his ideas, insinuating that they would be subject to disciplinary action if they did not. He also crafted a policy manual on what faculty should and should not do, without input from faculty. As one participant said, "Rather than using proven university processes to move faculty, he brought his political skills to bear to get a desired result. That was a very huge clash." In short, he did not respect preexisting institutional processes and acted as if he had unilateral authority.

Oscar at Overland State University and Richard at Ridge State University also had poor faculty relations. Both presidents undertook unpopular reorganization and retrenchment plans. During three years of Oscar's presidency, the faculty and deans at Overland State left in record numbers—four out of every ten faculty members, and four out of five deans. Neither the deans nor the faculty felt like Oscar valued their input. As one faculty member said, "You get the impression that he thinks we're not smart enough to have credible input. . . . University faculty, who are the smartest minds in the world, are not going to tolerate that. While he was smart and capable, it is hard to fathom that he didn't understand that."

Senior Leadership

Also important to a president's effectiveness is a strong senior leadership team or cabinet. Again, all four presidents came up short. Several hired "yes men," others alienated senior administrators, all ended up isolated from honest and constructive feedback.

At Central Plains, Charlie made significant and sometimes controversial changes in the composition of the senior leadership team within his first six months. He hired a slate of new vice presidents, but many lacked experience in higher education. He also removed two long-serving, highly regarded satellite campus directors. As one participant observed, he "just didn't have the experience or the depth of knowledge to understand how to select people for very critical positions within the university."

Charlie and Richard at Ridge State University were seen as surrounding themselves with people who failed to question them and provided uninformed or ill-informed guidance. Richard promoted a senior administrator who was instrumental in proposing that Ridge State merge with a local community college to form a university. As one cabinet member said, "Richard got himself into real trouble when he took over. It allowed him to get off track. . . . Some people around him kept him from doing stupid things. Then they were gone, and he was surrounded by yes people, or, worse than that, people who let him do stupid things for their own reasons."

Case Study: *University of South Hogan*

University of South Hogan is a small, master's level institution located in a large state. Comprised of four colleges and three divisions, it offers more than twenty-five undergraduate majors leading to a bachelor's degree, thirteen master's degrees, and one education specialist degree. South Hogan's thriving online program accounts for more than half of the student body.

Howard's short tenure at South Hogan was fractured from the start. During the search process, the campus community received word of his failed presidency at another academic institution. The board had been split on whether to hire him but eventually followed the lead of an influential board member who lobbied for Howard's appointment.

Some campus leaders described Howard as a visionary with poor communication skills. They noted that his volatile personality may have been his real downfall. Described as defensive and combative, Howard publicly berated board members, demanded blind loyalty from his cabinet, and flew into fits of rage with staff. The proverbial last straw involved a disagreement over a proposed real estate deal involving a wealthy donor.

As Howard was nearing the end of his contract, he asked his vice presidents to speak with the board on his behalf. Reluctantly, the board agreed that if Howard outlined his goals and objectives for the next contract period, they would be willing to work with him. When Howard refused to put this in writing, the board—unwilling to compromise—relieved him of his duties.

To their detriment, Howard at the University of South Hogan and Oscar at Overland State University both alienated their cabinets. Howard grew increasingly aloof from his cabinet. As campus criticism mounted, he became more defensive with his vice presidents and demanded ever greater loyalty. As one cabinet member recalled, "He slowly alienated everyone, from his most loyal supporters on down, because he demanded unquestioning, blind, fall-on-your-sword-for-me loyalty. Even when they knew he was not doing the right thing."

At Overland, without any input from his cabinet, Oscar hired a new provost who came from overseas aristocracy. This provost treated the deans as if they were beneath him and denied tenure to several well-respected junior faculty members, thus enraging the faculty. This president did not take the advice or seek guidance from the long-serving and well-respected vice presidents. Eventually, since their opinions were ignored, the vice presidents stopped communicating with Oscar.

Board

Since the board almost always has responsibility for hiring and firing the president, board-president relations are a major factor in presidential derailments. While some presidents overlook this obvious point, others find themselves with a different board than the one that hired them. Especially at public institutions where board membership is determined by the political system—be it the governor, the legislature, or the electorate—presidents must pay attention to changes in board composition. Problems with board-president relations can stem from presidential attitudes, board shortcomings, and changes in board membership. Often, some combination of these factors leads to a president's demise.

Howard at University of South Hogan and Charlie at Central Plains State University both bumped into board roadblocks that ultimately derailed them. The board of the University of South Hogan had been split on whether to hire Howard. Strong support from an influential board member tipped the scales in his favor. So, Howard did not start with unified support from the board.

At South Hogan, the situation worsened when the board wanted to enter into a real estate agreement with a wealthy donor, and Howard did not believe it was in the university's best interests. Never one to shy away from a good fight, Howard publicly battled with the board members who supported the real estate deal. Howard got personal. He wrote jingles and drew cartoons of board members. He publicly berated the influential board member who had supported his appointment. He took his pitch to the public, asking community members to sign petitions supporting his leadership of the university. Not surprisingly, the deal failed. Unfortunately, it garnered extensive coverage from the local media, causing great consternation and turmoil among board members.

At Central Plains State University, Charlie's problems with the board began when the composition changed radically during his tenure, especially when the chair, who had been one of his major proponents, was replaced. Charlie did not help himself by ignoring the board's authority. As one board member said, "It wasn't a relationship that was mutually beneficial, meaning he basically decided he would lead the way he wanted to lead and the board was merely an official body. . . . Despite how they would go about it, he would still do his own thing."

In working with the board, Charlie failed to understand the boundaries of his presidential authority and the importance of ensuring that the board was on board with his vision for Central Plains. He acted as though he did not have to answer to anyone, including the board. One participant noted that Charlie "clearly made his own decisions. He didn't consult the board in major decisions that were being made, and he didn't feel like he needed to." In an attempt to allow Charlie to continue as president, the board worked with him to renegotiate his duties. However, even after changes were made, Charlie was suspended and later relieved of his duties because of continuing conflicts with the board.

The State System and Government

Public universities operate within two larger structures, the first is the state system of higher education, which often has a centralized administration and a single board that oversees multiple institutions. The second is the state government that funds the university system. These two very important constituencies complicate the president's leadership and limit his autonomy because they have ultimate authority over the institutions. Two of the four derailed presidents ignored this reality.

At Ridge State University, Richard had compounding problems with the central administration of the state system. Within eight months of taking office, he was publicly named as a finalist for another presidency, which caused friction with the central administration that only grew worse. He was also an outspoken opponent of the system and took actions, such as disputing Ridge State's mission and exploring a merger with a community college.

At Central Plains State University, Charlie had trouble working with the state legislature, even though he had been closely connected to it in the past. In fact, the board had initially favored his strong "political connections." His adversarial nature, however, soon made some strong enemies. Central Plains state funding was reduced during his tenure.

Alumni, Donors, and the Community

Public universities do not exist in a vacuum. They depend on the good will and support—financial and political—of a community that includes alumni, donors, and the surrounding area. To their detriment, two of the four derailed presidents did not nurture these important constituents. Town-gown relationships colored events at Ridge State University and Overland State University. At Ridge State, Richard got into a bitter public disagreement with a neighborhood association about building student residences in the community.

Oscar at Overland State University did not participate in the town's civic life, which previous presidents had embraced. As one participant explained, "He really didn't get out into the community. There wasn't a strong community base to say 'I saw Oscar downtown, or at church, or at the Rotary meeting.'" So, during contentious moments, he had no community allies to rally to his support.

Nor did Oscar reach out to Overland's alumni and major donors. Several participants explained that donors did not feel as though Oscar respected them as rural people. One participant said, "I'd had several donors tell me, 'I will never give another dollar to the university. That man is a maniac, or that man treated me like I didn't count.'"

DERAILMENT THEME: POOR INTERPERSONAL SKILLS

A university president needs to be able to work well with a variety of people. Oscar, Richard, and Howard were plagued by problems with interpersonal relationships ranging from hot tempers and stubbornness to poor listening skills and a tendency for off-the-cuff comments. Often, the presidents' personalities got in their way. Eventually, these problems created an atmosphere of distrust and dislike that was insurmountable.

At Overland State University, Oscar was renowned for making arrogant, brash, shoot-from-the-hip comments when talking to the media and to key constituencies. Oscar liked to be challenged and "needed an enemy." Because he saw issues only in black and white, this often led to direct confrontations, which he seemed to relish. Another participant reflected, "I came to believe that Oscar loved controversy. If things were going smoothly, he wasn't comfortable. He just liked controversy."

Oscar talked at people, not with them. As one participant observed: "He had little patience for listening to other people. If you asked to meet with him about something, he would talk for 95 percent of the time, and you'd have to really whisk to get your question in before he was out of time." Oscar got in his own way, as another participant explained: "He was the most visionary individual I had ever met. He had a lot of excellent ideas for what a university could be and where it could go. But, he could not translate that into action because of his personality. He just didn't stop talking."

Howard, at the University of South Hogan, was stubborn and volatile. He was easily excitable and would fly into fits of rage. Sometimes, he ignored members of his cabinet. Other times he publicly castigated them. He often called employees after hours to vent his frustrations or to chastise them about something that had happened during the day. One participant recalled, "Typically, his timing was dreadful. I would get those calls on Friday afternoon at 5 o'clock. An hour of tirades made your weekend so wonderful."

Howard did not trust his colleagues and subordinates, nor they him. Remembering an altercation, one participant said that Howard accused him of "trying to drive him crazy" and sabotaging his bid for the presidency.

DERAILMENT THEME: ETHICAL LAPSES
Richard's derailment from Ridge State University involved ethical issues. He was perceived as dishonest and fiscally irresponsible. That combination was fatal. He was apt to make quick denials when caught off guard with damaging news and criticism. Richard spearheaded an unpopular faculty retrenchment plan during the early months of his presidency. When faculty spoke out against the plan, he disclaimed ownership of it. As one participant recalled, "His first reaction was to say, 'That was not my plan. It was just a draft.' It was a quick denial. Not only did this undermine his relationship with the faculty, but it also called into question his credibility."

Denying his hand in creating the faculty retrenchment plan may have been the first incident, others followed. When a newspaper published an article about his candidacy for another presidency, said a participant, "He just denied it, and then he tried to put some spin on it. We were not only taken aback by this news, but also taken aback by the glib denial, which made us question his credibility, which came back to haunt him in a bigger way." One participant described the departure of several administrators who left the university during his tenure because they felt that Richard was not "being honest in his statements and proclamations to the community." Richard soon lost the confidence of important constituencies.

His credibility was also called into question by his inability to stay within the university's budget. Under his leadership, the Ridge State's budget was overspent by several million dollars. Eventually, the board of the Ridge State University Foundation restricted his access to discretionary funds. While his profligate spending was problematic, the proverbial last straw was funding, that he claimed was promised, for an educational center that never materialized. According to one participant, Richard "brought in a potential donor and promised a lot of money. When the money wasn't there, he lied about it. The board felt that he had lost all credibility." This incident was widely covered in local and national newspapers, with assertions that Richard had deceived the state system and the campus community.

As one participant summed it up: "at the university level, some of these things—including and especially that last straw with lying about having the money—imperiled the faculty in particular. . . . There were moves afoot among the faculty. Some of them had directly contacted people at the central office. It was a classic erosion of confidence." A president with questionable ethics and severely damaged credibility is not viable as a campus leader. Ultimately, the state system released him from his duties as president.

Conclusion

While many lessons can be gleaned from these derailed presidents, the most notable one is that institutional fit between a president and a university is of paramount importance. As the chief executive officer, the president is not just a figurehead but also a cheerleader and advocate on behalf of the institution. To succeed in these roles, he must embrace and embody the university's mission and culture. The institution has to "fit" the president and vice versa. When smart, visionary presidents find the right institution, great things can happen. But, as illustrated in these case studies, a mismatch erodes confidence from the faculty, staff, and community.

Second, universities are built around a culture that values democratic principles and consensus building. Constituents expect, and sometimes demand, open dialogue between presidents, board, faculty, and staff—not just during executive transitions but throughout a president's tenure. A president's communication style, as well as the substance of his message, shapes his relationship with constituents. The more open and straightforward the president is, the more willing his constituents are likely to be. At all four universities, the presidents were described as listening too little. Effective leaders listen more than they talk. Building consensus and articulating a vision for a university requires communicating—in all directions—with a wide variety of constituencies.

Finally, all four presidents did, in fact, do good things for their institutions. Most participants were quick to point out good qualities, characteristics, and ideas that the presidents implemented while in office. No one said that they were not qualified to be leaders. But, somewhere along the way, they did something to erode campus confidence and could no longer lead the university forward.

Chapter Four

Presidential Derailments at Public Research Universities

Keith Carver

Nature of Public Research Universities

Public research universities offer undergraduate, graduate, and doctoral degrees in a wide range of disciplines, including science, engineering, technology, mathematics, humanities, and the social sciences. Many also offer professional programs in law, business, education, engineering, public policy, and social work. Some also have medical or veterinary schools.

Their cultures are complex because their settings and missions are complex. Many public research universities are part of larger systems comprised of one or more research universities and other comprehensive campuses. They tend to be the largest enrollment campuses in the state and operate with the largest budgets, even though state appropriations are a declining percentage of revenues for many research universities. The expectations of faculty do not overlook the need for competent and caring teaching at every level, but the ascendant expectation of faculty is on research and publication. Faculty governance mechanisms such as senates tend to be active and vocal. They are usually home to highly visible and highly expensive intercollegiate athletic programs. This context of mission complexity, active internal and external governance stakeholders, and program service duties to citizens of the state and to national and global clients marks them as organizations of majestic complexity and leadership challenge.

Derailment Themes

This chapter examines derailment themes that emerged from case studies at four public, research universities that experienced an executive derailment (see table 4.1).

Five derailment themes emerged from the case studies, as shown in table 4.2. These case studies are based on confidential interviews with participants with firsthand knowledge of the derailment, and their names and institutional details have been disguised to maintain their anonymity.

DERAILMENT THEME: ETHICAL LAPSES

Unethical behavior—observed or perceived—contributed to two of the executive derailments of public research universities. Sally at University of the

Table 4.1.   Profile of research universities case studies

Characteristic	State University of the North	University of the Southeast	University of the East	Western State University
			Institution	
Student enrollment	45,000	42,000	17,000	21,000
Student-to-faculty ratio	32:1	32:1	17:1	16:1
Professional programs	Law, veterinary medicine, education, engineering	Law, veterinary medicine, education, engineering	Veterinary medicine	Law, medicine
Single or multiple campuses	Multiple	Multiple	Single	Single
Research partnerships	Federal (energy)	Federal (energy)	Federal (NASA)	Various regional
Extension services	Agriculture, public service	Agriculture, public service	Agriculture	Agriculture, public policy
Governance structure	Appointed by governor	Appointed by governor	Appointed by governor	Appointed by governor
Length of board terms (years)	6	6	9	6
Length of service of derailed leader (years)	1	1.5	2	1

Table 4.2   Derailment themes at public research universities

Theme	Sally at University of the Southeast	Nicholas at State University of the North	Edward at University of the East	Walter at Western State University
	President			
Poor interpersonal skills	X	X	X	X
Inability to lead key constituencies	X	X		
Board shortcomings	X	X	X	X
Ethical lapses	X	X		
Difficulty adapting	X		X	X

Southeast was involved in an inappropriate relationship with a subordinate and Nicholas at the State University of the North was fiscally irresponsible and misused university resources for personal benefit.

CASE STUDY: *Southern University of the Southeast*

University of the Southeast is a large public, land grant university with a multicampus system. It has a research partnership with a municipal power entity and a public service program that extends into every county in the state.

Sally, the derailed president, followed a long-tenured, revered president. Once in office, Sally quickly brought in a new cabinet of senior advisors. Although accomplished individuals in their respective fields, they had limited experience in higher education or state service and were reluctant to challenge the president publicly or behind the scenes.

Sally quickly found herself under political pressure to reorganize the university. As an alumni leader explained, "Sally was chosen to 'do the deed' in the university." But, she was ill-prepared for the negative response when she presented a radical plan for reorganizing University of the Southeast. Her plan included the elimination of the chancellor's position for the research university campus in the system, with the system president serving as both system and campus executive. The plan caused uneasiness across the system, especially in some of the far-flung campuses. Her plan also included restructuring the university's athletic program, which alienated not only students and alumni but also the state general assembly. Her cabinet had given her little constructive feedback, and she had not vetted the plan in advance.

The final straw came when news broke of an alleged affair between Sally and a staff member. Within the campus, this suggestion of an inappropriate relationship was widely known. But, when news of this purported relationship moved into a public forum on the front page of the local newspaper, Sally's departure became inevitable. She resigned, which avoided certain board action to relieve her of duty.

At University of the Southeast, Sally's ethical lapses were of a personal nature. Simply put, she had an alleged inappropriate relationship with a subordinate. While not confirmed, the stigma surrounding the relationship was damaging to her presidency. A participant explained, "There was one primary factor, and that was personal misbehavior. It was widely known that there was an in-office relationship that was inappropriate and ultimately corrupt." It is exceedingly difficult, if not impossible, for a board to support a president who lacks personal integrity. Such obvious ethical lapses cannot be explained or defended. As a board member said, "Sally gave into things that she shouldn't have. . . . She was not as strong a leader as we had hoped she would be."

DERAILMENT THEME: BOARD SHORTCOMINGS

Board and search process shortcomings played into the presidential derailments of all four of these public research universities. In particular, they had fundamentally flawed search processes. Many institutions of higher education rely on search firms and consulting groups to recruit a pool of qualified candidates for the chief executive officer position, but ultimate responsibility for hiring the president rests with the board. Unfortunately, the boards of these four institutions did not sufficiently examine the candidates' past personal and professional behaviors. While boards certainly bear some burden for numerous derailments, the research associated with public, research universities show that this blame is also shared with university officials, search firms, and even governmental agencies. That being said, this research suggests that derailments at large universities are often the culmination of flawed search processes.

CASE STUDY: *State University of the North*

State University of the North is a large, multicampus, public university system that offers more than three hundred degree programs. It has nationally recognized professional programs in law, veterinary medicine, education, and engineering. It has strong ties to federal, state, county, and city governments. It has a research partnership with a federal energy agency and it also operates an extended public service agency that offers services and programs to every city and county governmental entity in the state.

Nicholas, the derailed president of the State University of the North, followed another derailed president. Wanting an expedient transition, the board hired Nicholas after a national search process. When Nicholas arrived on campus, the institution was still recovering from ethical misbehavior of a previous president and his involuntary departure.

Nicholas had a reputation as an arrogant, aloof chancellor with a sense of entitlement. He lived large on the university's dime. Nicholas made headlines when a local newspaper reported misuse of state-funded equipment for personal reasons. This led to further investigations that revealed an array of expenses, charged to State University of the North, for luxury home items.

As the internal and external support dwindled amidst the controversy, the board stepped into action. The governor, as chair of the board, and the vice chair met with Nicholas to discuss the situation, and Nicholas resigned immediately.

The search process at State University of the North was described as a classic example of Murphy's law: Anything that could have gone wrong, did. First, interview participants claimed that the presidential search was conducted in haste to remove the bad taste from problems with the previous president. "State University failed Nicholas and failed itself by selecting him. For whatever reason, through the search and orientation processes, they failed to inform him of the environment he was going to land in," according to a participant. Second, the integrity of the process was sorely undermined. Although he denied the claims, there were allegations that Nicholas was given the interview questions in advance and met with key government leaders prior to the formal interview.

In contrast to Sally of University of the Southeast above, Nicholas's ethical lapses were of a different nature. An extravagant president with a sense of entitlement, he spent the public university's money on personal luxury items. This was not new behavior on his part. Before coming to the University of the North, he had previously served as president of another public university. At this university, Nicholas had accepted several gifts—including large amounts of cash—from corporations and other organizations. After news of his misuse of University of the North resources for personal use became public, further investigations revealed that he had not followed state purchasing policy on other expenditures. "He didn't want to keep receipts. He just wanted to spend money," a cabinet member explained. At the meeting immediately following the chancellor's resignation, much of the discussion focused on Nicholas's financial decisions. The board established more stringent internal control policies, such as more frequent audits of expenditures, well-defined policies for the president's entertainment expenses, and a direct line of communication between the auditors, fiscal officers of the university, and the board.

University of the Southeast also had a flawed search process. The guardians of the search did not pay attention to concerns expressed by the campus community. An advisory committee comprised of alumni, faculty, staff, and students did not recommend Sally for the president's position. An alumni representative suggested that the board of the University of the Southeast settled for Sally because, "The pool was weak, and we didn't get any outstanding candidates." As a board member explained, "When we selected her, we did some background checks and thought that she was the person for the job. . . . Obviously, it didn't turn out the way that we had hoped."

DERAILMENT THEME: INABILITY TO LEAD KEY CONSTITUENCIES

Especially at public universities, the president must coordinate a diverse group of constituents. Both Sally at University of the Southeast and Nicholas at University of the North ran into difficulties with multiple constituents. Sally did a poor job of selecting senior advisors for her cabinet. Sally's detachment from the campus communities at Southeast and insulation from public perception was compounded by an ineffective cabinet. She did not cultivate a team of advisors in whom she could confide or who would tell her uncomfortable things she needed to know about her leadership or institutional problems at the university.

Faculty and staff at Southeast noted that Sally selected unqualified people to assist in carrying out her reorganization plan. Some of them came from out of state, several came from government and private industry, and few were experienced academic administrators. A faculty member attributed some of her derailment to "a couple of bad judgments on the personnel side." These advisors did not give the president good advice, nor did they help educate her about the idiosyncrasies of Southeast's culture and circumstances.

At State University of the North, Nicholas also showed a lack of good judgment in selecting his closest advisors, many of whom did not seem to be well qualified for their positions. An administrator also described "a degree of nepotism" in his decisions. Commenting on Nicholas's struggling public image barely a year into the president's tenure, the governor suggested that Nicholas needed to be more open and cooperative with institutional stakeholders.

Derailment Theme: Poor Interpersonal Skills

All four of these derailed presidents had problems with interpersonal relationships. Their attitudes and styles, as well as their actions, created tension or conflict between the president and the greater university community.

Case Study: *University of the East*

University of the East is a midsized, land grant university that offers 175 programs leading to bachelor's, master's, specialist, and doctoral degrees. It is the largest public university in the state and contains the state's only veterinary medicine program With an active extension program that operates offices across the state, Eastern has a tradition steeped in providing leadership and service to the agricultural community.

Described as a closed-door process, the board kept the search somewhat private in order to protect the confidentiality of the candidates, who were currently employed and therefore did not want to be publicly identified. Four finalists emerged, but none of them had unanimous board support. Edward surfaced as a last-minute candidate after private consultation with members close to the search committee. With little and late input from the campus community, his appointment was a surprising choice. He was not experienced in higher education. With an executive background in government service, he brought strong operational management skills. Decisive and in the habit of being in charge, he was used to working in a bureaucratic environment that moved quickly when necessary.

Accustomed to giving orders and having them followed, Edward did not adjust to consensual decision making and the engagement of multiple stakeholders and did not receive well criticism from faculty decision bodies. He was not able to appreciate the merit of honest dissent so essential to any organizational climate but certainly so in a university.

Edward's top-down management style was not well received at University of the East. A couple of initial missteps included a controversial decision regarding a campus beautification project and a heated reaction in the form of a multiple page memo when he was criticized by the faculty for issues of shared governance.

Nor did Nicholas at State University of the North relate well to faculty and staff. His elitist attitude and extravagant lifestyle were not in keeping with a state university known for its commitment to small businesses and middle class values. As one faculty member stated, "Nicholas had an agenda for what he wanted to do at State, but his arrogance kept him from being effective."

Sally, at the University of the Southeast, also came off as unapproachable and aloof. Her predecessor, an affable and outgoing man, pointed out their different styles: "Sally's approach to things was to go off in a corner. If you wanted to see her, you went over to her." Because Sally instilled a sense of fear among her staff, this was particularly problematic. As one participant explained, "When you're at the top, you carry a big sword and have all the power. People are afraid to tell you something that they think you don't want to hear, and I saw some of that going on with Sally. We all went through it. In one way, we wanted to tell her, 'Stop it. You don't know how this is being perceived.' In another way, we couldn't tell her. She was the boss. She could fire us."

Derailment Theme: Difficulty Adapting

The inability to change or adapt to the culture of a new university contributed to three of the four derailments. Organizational culture derives from a long history of shared experiences. The customs, practices, values, and attitudes that evolve among constituents of a particular university must be recognized and respected by the chief executive officer of the organization. Only after demonstrating an understanding and appreciation of the institution should a president attempt significant organizational changes. Ignoring campus traditions, Nicholas, Sally, and Edward neither appreciated the magnitude of the president's leadership responsibilities nor learned how to work within the academic institutional structure that included governing boards and a state system.

Case Study: *Western State University*

Western State University is a public land grant university system that offers more than 180 degree programs at the bachelor's, master's, and doctoral levels. It also offers professional programs in law and medicine. It operates from a single campus situated in a rural area.

From the start, Walter, the derailed chancellor, seemed overwhelmed by the responsibilities of his position. He moved from an administrative position at a school of about 1,500 students to a university of 21,000 and from a campus with no union presence to one with a union. He was relatively unengaged with the community and did little to build bridges with community and civic stakeholders.

Walter became known for being late to meetings and was often a "no show" at important university events, behaviors which did not reflect a high degree of responsibility on the part of an executive.

As a note of background, the university had experienced an excessive number of derailments over a period spanning almost twenty years.

Walter, at Western State University, lacked the leadership skills to succeed as president and was ill equipped to deal with the challenges of the new role. According to a senior administrator, "Early on, it was clear that he did not understand or handle the expectations of the office. He was simply not prepared for the job."

At University of the Southeast, Sally embarked on a major reorganization that was a radical departure from the traditional organizational structure. Her plan created a sense of uneasiness across the university system, and people feared that one regional institution might "drop off the face of the earth." From the perspective of faculty and administrators, her plan seemed to be presented and implemented without much forethought or preparation. From the board perspective, Sally failed to anticipate the implications of and reaction to her plan. As a board member explained, "She tried to change the system. That scared lots of people." She also wanted to reorganize Southeast's athletic program, which rippled across the university, through the alumni community, and into the state assembly. As the board member concluded, "You need to change with the times, but you need to think about what you do."

The University of the East was Edward's first, and presumably last, foray into higher education. He had trouble adjusting from his federal, executive position to an academic setting. His top-down style did not transfer well to a university campus.

Conclusion

Ethical misbehaviors on the part of presidents or boards are and should be cause for derailment. Flawed and mismanaged search processes increase the probability of derailments. Finding the right style and personality "fit" between an institution and a president is also essential. One would not expect to find difficulty in interpersonal skills in a leader who had demonstrated sufficient promise to be considered for an executive level appointment such as a presidency, but it is clear from these cases, and previous cases from other institutions, that presidents can behave in infantile and insensitive ways with a range of their constituents.

Chapter Five

Presidential Derailments at Community Colleges

Leigh Ann Touzeau

The Nature of Community Colleges

According to the American Association of Community Colleges, there are nearly 1,200 community colleges in the United States, and they educate approximately 44 percent of all undergraduate students (American Association of Community Colleges, 2013). Community colleges share a common set of values and purposes: to serve diverse populations, to provide open access, to offer developmental education for underprepared students, and to respond to local community needs. Their diverse offerings include career and technical associate degrees, university transfer associate degrees, certificate programs, and continuing education.

Community colleges are dynamic institutions and a growing field. Their leadership changes frequently with an average 30 percent turnover every two years at the presidential level. About 75 percent of community college CEOs participating in a recent survey plan to retire in the next ten years, with another 15 percent eyeing retirement in eleven to fifteen years. These startling figures don't include involuntary departures (American Association of Community Colleges, 2012).

Derailment Themes

The analysis of derailment is not a fault-finding exercise; it is rare that the fault lies wholly with either the board or the president. The analytics repeatedly remind us of the delicate balance and intricate calculations that any president must maintain in order to thrive at any institution at any time. To outsiders, presidents may seem fairly powerful and autonomous. New presidents may fail to realize just how many and varied their stakeholders are, how power is distributed among them, and how difficult it is to retain political capital when tough decisions must be taken.

Four community colleges provided sufficient information about derailments to be perfect case studies (table 5.1). They are based on confidential interviews with participants with firsthand knowledge of the derailment, and their names and institutional details have been disguised to maintain their anonymity. While the specific events that led to these derailments were different, common causes emerged at the four institutions (table 5.2).

Derailment Theme: Inability to Lead Key Constituencies

In order to succeed, a community college president needs strong working relationships with key constituencies, including the board, faculty, government, and community leaders. The derailed presidents in these four cases all had difficulty collaborating with key constituencies. At Alpine, the president

Table 5.1.   Profile of community college case studies

	Institution			
Characteristic	Alpine Community College	Birch Community College	Cypress Community College	Dogwood Community College
Enrollment	56,000	4,000	2,100	13,000
Student-to-faculty ratio	25:1	20:1	20:1	23:1
Number of campuses	3	1	1	4
Governance	Local board, appointed by governor, serving 4–8 years	State/local board, half appointed by governor and half by county commissioner, serving 7–10 years total	Local board, appointed by governor, serving 4–8 years	Local board, elected by districts in target service area, serving 4–8 years
Faculty	Unionized	Unionized	Not unionized	Not unionized
Funding	State	State and county	State	State

Table 5.2.   Derailment themes at community colleges

| | President | | | |
Theme	Antonio at Alpine Community College	Brandon at Birch Community College	Calvin at Cypress Community College	Daniel at Dogwood Community College
Inability to lead key constituencies	X	X	X	X
Difficulty adapting	X	X	X	X
Poor interpersonal skills	X	X	X	

stood in the crosshairs between an aloof board and a powerful faculty. At Birch, the president took on the county commissioner. At Cypress, the president shook up the entire campus with a reorganization plan. At Dogwood, the president tangled with the faculty and, along the way, lost board support. These presidents failed to invest in building social and political capital before taking on notable campus challenges.

The Board

CASE STUDY: *Alpine Community College*

Alpine Community College is a large, urban, multicampus, public community college that offers several career technical programs and hundreds of college transfer courses through associate of science and arts degrees. Student enrollment is large and diverse across its three campuses.

Antonio was hired after the retirement of Zack, a respected and long-term president. Zack had been at Alpine for many years, having served as a faculty member prior to his appointment as president. Zack was a pillar of the community and had built strong relationships with board members over time.

Antonio relocated from another state for his first opportunity to serve as president. His pleasant demeanor and collaborative management style were notably different than that of his predecessor. His approach to working with faculty was participatory, and he sought their opinions on such issues as new programs and faculty hires. This unnerved some board members, especially because the board had always maintained a certain distance from the strong faculty union.

Ultimately, no single event led to Antonio's derailment. Rather, Antonio had recurring problems working with an overpowering and micromanaging board and adjusting to Alpine's culture, especially its power structure and decision-making style. He also failed to communicate his vision for the college and missed critical opportunities to involve others in being part of that vision.

Antonio's downfall at Alpine was firmly rooted in board problems. According to a vice president, board members assumed that they would be able to tell Antonio what to do. Traditionally, the Alpine board had been very active in the day-to-day workings of the college. Upon his arrival, Antonio tried to rectify this by establishing clear boundaries between the board's governance role and his executive authority. When board members began actively trying to make administrative decisions, such as construction contract awards and dean appointments, Antonio realized he was in trouble. In the spirit of collaboration, he invited one of the most rambunctious board members to serve on the dean's search committee. This was the beginning of the end.

Antonio's derailment was instigated by two board members who, ironically, had lobbied to hire him. They had expected him to be beholden to them. As one board member lamented, "It was a sad situation because, right from the beginning, we had two renegade board members trying to get their way and run the college."

When asked, in hindsight, what Antonio could have done differently, a board member suggested, "Upfront, he should have asked what the board's expectations were of him and what his expectations were of the board in order to see if everyone was on the same page. . . . Then he could have asked, 'What can the board do to help me be successful?' "

Government Representatives

CASE STUDY: *Birch Community College*

Birch Community College is a single campus, comprehensive community college that offers transfer and technical degree programs. It is located in a suburban area, and its student population is fairly homogenous.

Brandon followed a long-term, well-liked president and was also a first-time president from out of state. Brandon's derailment had one precipitating event—a very public battle with the county commissioner over how to allocate funds from a multimillion-dollar legal settlement. With encouragement from the board and widespread community support, Brandon lobbied hard for the money to renovate a dilapidated building on campus. The county commissioner, however, wanted to renovate one of the buildings under her jurisdiction. The debate between Brandon and the county commissioner was covered extensively in the local media and became very contentious.

While Brandon's derailment can be traced directly to a feud with the county commissioner, several other factors also contributed to his early departure. Brandon had difficulty building good relationships with key constituents, not only the county commissioner individually but the community more broadly. He was perceived as an "outsider, arrogant, and snobby," and the community did not see him as one of their own.

But Brandon's main problem at Birch Community College was his relationship—or lack thereof—with the county commissioner, who appointed half of the board and represented one of two funding sources. The new county commissioner was elected during Brandon's second year of tenure, had a great deal of power in the community, and was very vocal about many issues. When it came time to appoint new trustees, she used her authority to make certain that her appointees knew she could no longer work with Brandon. Eventually, she appointed a new board member and influenced enough of the other board members to result in the termination of Brandon's contract.

A faculty member reflected, "The only thing that he did wrong was care about the college too much. All of his actions were to support the college. We really needed that new building. But, with the political atmosphere in Birch, there was no way he was going to win once she made it a fight." Brandon's departure started with his highly visible confrontation with the county commissioner, which carried over into his problems working with the board.

Multiple Constituents

Case Study: *Cypress Community College*

Cypress Community College is a single campus community college that offers several transfer, technical, and certificate programs. The relatively small student body is fairly homogeneous. The campus, located in a tourist community, is noted for an extremely laid-back culture.

When Calvin took on the presidency, the board told him that Cypress needed a "change agent." Calvin had a strong personality with a demanding and aggressive management style. As the new president, Calvin really shook up the college.

Calvin made enemies of some very powerful people, upsetting the college's tightly knit culture and town-gown relationships. Within his first two years, half of the faculty had been fired or quit. He did not renew the contract of a top administrator whose family's construction company had, literally, built the town. Nor did he choose a local construction company for the bid to build new dorms on campus. At a dinner party, he threw a drink in a colleague's face.

In the end, he had difficulty working not just with staff and faculty but also with the board. He was described as a bully, demeaning, and even crazy, which made him not only difficult to work for but also an easy target for critics. Eventually, an anonymous e-mail campaign calling for his resignation succeeded.

At Cypress, Calvin had a mixed record on working with constituents. He had strong advocates and equally strong and numerous detractors. As a board member explained, "You either liked him, or you hated him. There wasn't much in between." Ultimately, those who did not had the power to derail him.

Cypress is a small community whose members enjoyed close ties, and Calvin did not make a concerted effort to keep those around him content or to pay close attention to the local power structure. As a vice president noted, "He didn't renew the contract of a senior administrator whose family's construction company built this town. So, then the administrator organized a meeting of upset employees with one of the board members without Calvin knowing." This conflict of interest should have been addressed by the board.

In his determination and excitement for getting things done, Calvin made enemies of some powerful people at the college and within the community. A vice president observed, "He didn't understand the people he was going up against in this community and how resistant to change and complacent the faculty and staff had become. He thought he could just come in and make all these widespread changes that fast without making anyone upset. Not so."

After two years, when a vacated board position was filled by someone with ties to non-supporters, Calvin saw the writing on the wall. Knowing he lacked the votes to keep his job, he started to negotiate his departure.

Faculty

Case Study: *Dogwood Community College*

Dogwood Community College is a multicampus community college and serves a large geographic region. The student body is highly diverse, as are the course offerings. As president of Dogwood, Daniel followed a long-term, well-liked president at a community college with an entrenched way of doing things and a well-established hierarchy of power. The faculty had considerable power and, de facto, ran the institution. The board tried to keep the faculty happy and at a distance.

Daniel stepped into the middle of this delicate imbalance of power. After examining faculty job descriptions, he questioned whether the faculty was actually accomplishing all of the duties outlined in their job descriptions. For example, the job descriptions, which had not been updated in some time, listed academic advising of students, but very few faculty members actually did this. This challenge about their duties from the president's office was not well received by the faculty.

Having failed to cultivate strong relationships with board members, Daniel was in a weak position when the faculty crusade for his resignation reached the board level. When the faculty put forth a vote of no confidence, Daniel's tenure at Dogwood was destined for derailment.

At Dogwood, the domino affect of constituent relationships was also in play. Daniel had difficulty working with two key constituencies, first the faculty and then the board. After a short fourteen months, his presidency ended because of a no-confidence vote by the faculty. The faculty wielded their power over Dogwood Community College with pride. As a former vice president recounted, "I met a long-time, powerful, faculty member at a social gathering, and she made a point of letting me know how she had gotten rid of someone that she didn't like at the college. She ended up being the one who led the no-confidence vote against Daniel."

The board yielded to the faculty's desires. As a board member explained, "The board tried to placate the faculty, to keep the faculty happy and at arm's length. They didn't want to be bothered. So, when the faculty held a vote of no confidence, the board did nothing to support Daniel. It was a sad state of affairs." This passive board behavior may have been exacerbated by the lack of turnover on the board. Some trustees had served on the board for more than twenty years. Yet again, a derailed president's failure to work with one key constituency, in this case the faculty, led to fatal problems with the board, in this case with its own troubling behavior.

Derailment Theme: Difficulty Adapting

The second derailment theme involves the failure of the president to adapt or change to the culture of the college and that of the community. Some interesting similarities exist among all four community college presidents. First, each derailed president followed a long-term, well-liked president. Second, this was the first presidency for each derailed president. Third, all of the presidents hailed from afar. In order to succeed, they needed to better understand, appreciate, and adjust to the cultural context of their colleges.

Circumstances beyond the President's Control

Antonio's two long-term, beloved presidential predecessors were born and raised in the town of Alpine; the first had led the community college for fifteen years, and the one before him for eighteen. Brandon at Birch and Calvin at Cypress both followed presidents who had been promoted from within, knew all of the faculty and staff, and had lived in their respective communities for many years. Daniel at Dogwood followed a former president who had previously served as the chief academic officer and had been at the college for more than twenty years.

These institutional circumstances are beyond the control of the incoming president, but that does not negate them. Reflecting a common sentiment, a faculty member from Birch admitted, "We didn't trust him at first because he didn't seem like he was one of us. We were used to the former president, and it took us some time to get to know him. Some faculty never really gave him a chance."

Getting to Know the Culture and the Community

Being an outsider does not necessarily lead to a presidential derailment, but it does require the newcomers to pay careful attention to local politics, college customs, and preexisting relationships. In these case studies, the out-of-towners also failed to understand institutional culture and to appreciate the importance of cultivating local support. For example, Antonio did not take into account the "comfortable distance" between the board and faculty that was deeply engrained in Alpine's culture. As a board member observed, "Our last president had been there for years, he grew up here, he knew the local politics, understood the board, knew the faculty, and understood the salary negotiations with the union. He knew how to keep the board informed, but not too involved."

As president, Brandon failed to adapt his personal leadership style to the culture of Birch Community College and the broader community. Birch is located is a small industrial town where most citizens were not educated past high school. Little details were noticed. One board member commented: "Look at him—with those cuff links—who does he think he is?" Brandon's way of dressing may have made it easier for the community to not accept Brandon as one of their own. This, in turn, made it easier for the county commissioner to portray him as an outsider "who didn't know what was best for the community."

The Challenge of Change

Presidents brought in with a mandate for change have to overcome even stronger resistance as outsiders. As a board member from Alpine acknowledged, "Antonio was from another state school, and some faculty and board members complained that he wasn't like Zack. You can't ask a person to come in and be a change agent but act exactly like the last guy. It just doesn't work that way."

Calvin faced similar challenges at Cypress Community College, located in a small town with a tight-knit community and entrenched power structures. By most accounts, he was a lightning rod for a college and a community that were not ready for such a fast and furious pace of change. One board member stated, "We brought him in to turn this place around. We were on the state's 'critical concern' list because of declining enrollments, and we needed someone who wasn't afraid of change. After his first year, about half the full-time faculty was gone—either he had fired them or they had just left. He boosted enrollment, got us a new website, landed a million-dollar grant, and was really a mover and a shaker. But you can't just let all those people go and expect them to be happy about it. He did too much too fast."

Similarly, Daniel wanted to implement change at Dogwood, but he did not understand the extraordinary power of the faculty and their past involvement in major campus initiatives. As a faculty member reflected, "He was a good person with good ideas, he just didn't ask us to be involved enough. If he had gotten some of the most powerful faculty on his side, he could have done anything. But, the second he made them mad, he was gone."

DERAILMENT THEME: POOR INTERPERSONAL SKILLS

All of the derailed presidents had problems with interpersonal relationships with their colleagues at the community college. In some instances, they also generated many favorable comments about their character, collaborative nature, and constructive changes championed at the institution. However, they each had some weakness that made it particularly difficult for them to relate to others, and this weakness contributed to their eventual derailment.

Perceptions and Posturing: Confidence versus Arrogance

Antonio's problems with interpersonal relationships became more evident as time passed. According to one staff member, he especially seemed to falter when he came under fire: "He could be quite stubborn. Once he made up his mind, you were not going to dissuade him. It wasn't even about being right. It seemed to be about winning. I think they call it machismo. He could be egotistical sometimes and defensive."

In Birch, faculty and staff described Brandon as snobby and difficult to approach. As a board member observed, "The way that Brandon conducted himself—his confidence and his overall look (he was always dressed to the nines)—caused some locals to be suspicious of him. He was slick, and I think that he was perceived as disingenuous. I remember telling him, 'You can't say it that way. You need to be nicer.' But it is hard to change who you are."

Presidential Power Plays: Demanding and Demeaning

Board, administrative, and faculty members all commented on Calvin's strong personality. He was described as demanding, demeaning, and downright hostile. He had a reputation as a bully and reportedly used offensive language regularly. An article in the local newspaper noted: "Former and current college employees and faculty have accused the president of verbal and mental abuse, paranoia and having a 'hit list' of employees he wants gone. Some have called him 'crazy.' "

A board member articulated the creative tension at play: "He was exciting, he was a change agent, it is what we needed . . . He was doing what he thought was needed to move the college in the right direction, but he should have toned down his personality a bit. I think he just got too excited by his own level of power."

Conclusion

None of the community college presidents in these cases acted unethically or selfishly. Each worked to advance their institutions, but they had to contend with problematic boards—one that micromanaged, two that were heavily swayed by the faculty, and one that was strongly influenced by a government representative. In hindsight, these boards could or should have provided more guidance, support, and perhaps cover for the presidents they tasked with leading institutional change. At the same time, each president exhibited behaviors that doomed his tenure and negatively affected his relationship with key constituents, particularly faculty and board members.

In public institutions, external political realities inevitably shape the role and nature of a presidency. This was especially true for the derailed presidents of these four community colleges. George Bernard Shaw's observation that "all progress depends on the unreasonable man" may not hold true for presidencies in higher education.

Chapter Six

Firsthand Experiences of Derailed Presidents

Editors' Note

Every derailment is complicated and complex; it is almost inevitable that principals and observers will have different views on causation, different recollections of events, different views about the personalities involved, and different conclusions about culpability. Most derailments are shrouded in confidentiality. In these circumstances, it is nearly impossible to derive any lessons that might help either boards or presidents navigate their relationship.

In this chapter, two derailed presidents—William Frawley and Michael Garrison—share their experiences. Their candid commentary as principals is intended to be instructive without necessarily being dispositive. Publication in this volume of essays by two derailed presidents who were free to write and agreed to do so is for illustrative purposes. Their essays are quite different, as were the circumstances of their particular derailments. Their inclusion provides additional texture to the overall discussion. It is not an endorsement of the accounts rendered or the views expressed. Instruction, not judgment, is the aim and sole implication.

———————

The Personal Becomes Public
William Frawley, University of Mary Washington
(2006–2007)

Founded in 1908, the University of Mary Washington is a small, public master's level institution located within an hour of Washington, D.C., and Richmond, Virginia. In 2007, William Frawley was terminated by the board of visitors—comprised of twelve members appointed by the governor and confirmed by the Virginia General Assembly—following a widely publicized arrest for driving under the influence of alcohol, an example of a personal frailty leading to derailment.

Frawley had a distinguished record as a linguist and cognitive scientist. He had successfully held administrative positions at the University of Delaware and the George Washington University. As the faculty director for academic programs and planning at the University of Delaware, he oversaw the revamping of the core requirements for the College of Arts and Sciences. As a dean at the George Washington University, he had responsibility for more than forty academic departments. Frawley helped raise more than $45 million for George Washington's Columbian College of Arts and Sciences, and external funding from grants increased 28 percent during his tenure.

Mary Washington was Frawley's first presidency, and it lasted less than a year. During his brief tenure as president at the University of Mary Washington, Frawley created several scholarship programs, launched the wholesale reevaluation of the academic arena, and called on each department to develop a strategic plan outlining its goals and objectives. He crafted an agreement with the Naval Postgraduate School in Monterey, California, that would align both schools to work cooperatively on service, teaching, and scholarly activities.

According to the university's summary of his presidency, "The Frawley Administration oversaw many changes in administration as well as in student and campus life. New faculty with different ideas, technological advances, as well as a reevaluation of campus space, turned this period into one of change or at least of expected change. Monetary aspects were scrutinized and reassessed during this time as well, leading to long term plans being discussed and created involving finances and projected changes in the campus."

Frawley is currently living in Saudi Arabia, where he's a professor of English and linguistics at Qassim University.

What follows was written by William Frawley and published in the *Washington Post*—it is reprinted here with his permission. Following the *Post* essay is an update on the aftermath of Frawley's derailment; it consists of questions posed by Stephen Joel Trachtenberg and Gerald B. Kauvar and of Frawley's responses.

Frawley's Narrative

In our zero-tolerance times, when a public figure melts down, everyone wants answers—right now. Explain yourself, voices demand. Take responsibility!

But as someone who has suffered a calamitous breakdown, I know that anyone at the center of a public storm needs to comprehend what happened, move away from shame, and give a coherent account of events. In the meantime, the impulse to self-punish and angry demands for retribution from others help no one heal.

Earlier this year, while president of the University of Mary Washington in Fredericksburg [Virginia], I was, Lindsay Lohan–like, charged with two DUIs. But where Lohan and other celebrities are nourished by their public embarrassments, my meltdown cost me my job and may well have cost me my career. As I grapple with the aftermath, I wonder whether things had to turn out as they did and what lessons should be learned from my crisis.

As is true for most people, college presidents' behavior does not always match our ideals. But when we do something embarrassing, the gap between the two is highlighted and our sins are broadcast to all. Then, as Jeffrey Rosen wrote in his book *The Unwanted Gaze*, the public quickly mistakes mere information for genuine knowledge of our characters. But there's always more to the story, and that critical extra needs to be told openly and in its proper course. A rush to explanation is just as treacherous as a rush to judgment.

I came to the Presidency of Mary Washington in 2006 with a solid record of achievement: I had been a dean at George Washington University, published more than a dozen books and hundreds of papers and reviews, won recognition for my teaching, raised millions of dollars. But the way I left—with no apparent consideration for my illness or my record and no support for my family's transition to a new life—contrasted sharply with the exits of other university presidents in similar situations. What is shared with them was the realization that the first casualty in such crises—but the only thing that saves you in the end—is honesty.

My April meltdown was of my own making, as I have repeatedly acknowledged and publicly regretted. I've always said that I should not have been driving, and I'm thankful that I alone was hurt. I know my actions cracked the trust that the UMW board and community had placed in me. But their hard-edged reactions also cracked my trust in them.

For 45 years, I had self-treated a case of undiagnosed depression with compulsive work and, lately, alcohol. New heart problems and allergies added to the mix, as did the stress of separation from my own family, which remained in Maryland.

I wouldn't listen to those who urged me to slow down, and even foiled an arrangement by one of my vice presidents to get me to do so. I didn't want to know myself.

On April 10, I got up at 4:30 a.m., as always. Racing around, I was afraid I would be late for my autistic son's assessment in Bethesda, which I had already postponed twice. On the way there, I felt as though I was going to have a nervous breakdown. To calm down, I drank some wine (after taking allergy medication) before I got on the road.

I'd never driven to Bethesda from UMW before, and I took the wrong exit off I-495. Confused, distracted, and on a twisting road, I went off a curve and flipped the car. I recall little of what happened afterward, except for telling the emergency crew not to defibrillate me because of my history of Wolff-Parkinson-White syndrome, an electrical problem of the heart. That evening, I awoke in an intensive care unit of Inova Fairfax Hospital. I argued my way out, insisting that I had to work the next day. At 1 a.m., I drove back to Fredericksburg. I have no idea how I made it there in my exhausted and still-sedated state.

I got up again at 4:30 a.m., wrote some e-mails (which I later saw were gibberish) and went to work. My startled staff sent me home, but I couldn't rest. Jittery and consumed again with the feeling that I was about to have a breakdown or heart attack, I drove up to horse country, parked, took in the scenery and drank again. On the way home, I hit a pothole and blew a tire but continued on, sleepless and disoriented.

Thankfully, someone noticed my erratic driving and called the police, who surely thought I was a nut case heading into . . . well, the UMW president's driveway! Filled in by some of my staff who had shown up at the scene, the police recognized what was happening; they charged me with DUI but, more important, took me to the hospital.

The upshot of that 26-hour sequence was six days in the hospital, a newly diagnosed cardiac problem—and scandal. My story was splashed across the local and national newspapers and (endlessly, it seemed) on television and the radio. I felt relentless shame.

Two days out of the hospital, I traveled to Fredericksburg to give the board of trustees an explanation. The scene was Kafkaesque. I don't believe I told the story very well; nor did the board listen very well. UMW's legal counsel, a representative from the state attorney general's office, instructed the members to say nothing. They listened in preternatural silence without being able to ask any questions to help them understand my story. My attorneys had advised me to limit what I said, so I wasn't able to give a full account even if I had one.

Board members responded to my sincere questions—"Why would I throw away a 30-year career?" and "Why would I hurt such a good institution?"—with quizzically tilted heads. I asked them to allow me to begin treatment under a team of medical experts and not to act precipitously.

The university rector came to the president's house the next morning. Standing in the kitchen, I asked him whether I'd be able to preserve my tenure as a distinguished university professor. "They want you out of here," he said. I asked for a medical leave. "They don't want to do that," he replied. I would have to resign all association with UMW or be fired.

Ten days later, I accepted a severance package in exchange for my resignation. But in a surprise move, it was pulled off the table that same day, and I was fired. I was instantly left with no salary or benefits, no severance, no tenure. Our zero-tolerance times have seemingly produced no tolerance for tolerance.

I spent the summer in a deep depression even as I began six months of intensive treatments at clinics, hospitals, and an inpatient rehabilitation facility. On July 13, I accepted another board-approved severance—this one negotiated by an independent mediator. But in October, I learned that the state attorney general's office had rejected the settlement. The mediator was the only one more flabbergasted than I was.

The DUIs were resolved in September. My attorneys wanted me to go to trial, but I insisted on Alford pleas, a form of guilty plea. Justice was not blind to the extenuating circumstances of these incidents. My suspended sentence and fines and the loss of driving privileges in Virginia recognized that the DUIs were the culmination of a long, complicated series of events.

But the public reaction was mixed. Many faculty, students, community members, and even strangers wrote to me with sensitivity and expressing support. But many others wrote to the Fredericksburg newspapers suggesting that I had gotten off easy or had been handed a sweet deal. Letter writers compared me to Michael Vick and Virginia Tech shooter Hui Cho. If I read the letters correctly, it seemed that for many my first sin was not the DUIs but my reported salary as president.

In the push of public scrutiny, many observers cited their "right" to know details about my personal life. To what extend does the public have a right to know a public figure's medical history and personal past? When does the clamoring for personal information become mere prurient interest? The Fredericksburg *Free*

Lance-Star questionably dredged up a decades-old incident in which I had confronted a stalker who had harassed my wife for many years. I went from pillar to pilloried, and the debasing revealed a great deal about the community's expectations, social values and public and private faces.

Close on the heels of public humiliation came institutional erasure. I was immediately cut off from the UMW e-mail system and couldn't even receive the e-mail notice of my firing. At the board's summer retreat, the strategic plan I had set in motion—buying the nearby shopping center for major expansion, building a new facility at the Navy research site at Dahlgren, [Virginia]—were reaffirmed. But I was told that when someone asked who recommended the excellent retreat site and my name surfaced, others gestured to silence the speaker. I had become, Harry Potter-style, He-Who-Must-Not-Be-Named.

Some in situations similar to mine have outlived their disasters. In 2004, an Emory university vice president faced serious charges. He accepted responsibility, sought help, and eventually returned to his position. Wisely, the university allowed him to take leave for treatment. Blessed are the judicious.

Others like me have had their fractures brutally displayed. American University President Benjamin Ladner had to resign in 2005 because of alleged financial transgressions; in 1990 Richard Berendzen had also been forced to resign as AU president after being charged with a sexual misdemeanor. The firing and vehement self-defense of Eastern Michigan University's John Fallon—dismissed this past July purportedly for his handling of a campus rape and murder case—have reached the *Larry King* show. Yet these institutions, recognizing that trauma involves a whole family, offered severance package to ease the transition to a new life. Berendzen even returned to his tenured professorship.

But as I endure the vicious new cyber-punishment of permanent exposure on the Internet, I am challenged to remake my reputation while simultaneously denied the opportunity for redemption that I accorded others.

As a longtime teacher, I know there are lessons to be learned from my situation. I've learned that honesty can guide you through dissolution to hope. My family is no longer four people living alone together. My wife and I are committed to a new future. My pre-teen daughter endured teasing with grace and has grown in the process. Recently, she asked me how I was feeling. "Pretty down," I replied. Her response was full of insight: "Why don't you go to a meeting?"

Another lesson is that institutions must keep the past an open book and spread the wisdom gained from uncomfortable situations. But that doesn't mean we can't have regrets. UMW can speak for itself, but I regret losing the opportunity to help students, faculty, and staff discuss and deal with compulsion and substance issues. I regret, now that I'm healthy and my problems are cured or managed, that I can't teach and learn at UMW again. These are deep regrets from a permanent and painful loss.

Frawley Interview

We wanted an opportunity to add to Professor Frawley's op-ed piece to determine whether during the intervening years he had modified any of the views he expressed and to gain additional insight into the aftermath of a presidential derailment. Here are our questions and his answers.

Do you have any regrets about publishing the piece?

Not at all. Everything I wrote is completely true, and it is foolish to regret the truth, no matter how difficult the facts. Maybe to the surprise of many, I regret almost nothing of all the events, except for the pain I caused people, which I could have managed better. My life has always been lived almost totally forward, and regret suggests you wish things could have turned out otherwise. But much of what happened was in many ways in the cards. I have always found myself in situations rather than creating them, and I have never thought much of the, pardon the pun, "making and entering" view of experience. Ambition and "reach exceeding grasp" have not impressed me much. For fifty-eight years I have had essentially in-the-moment living. Regret does not survive well in that kind of life.

If you were to write something today about your experience, would it be different? How?

What do you mean? My sense now of that experience then? The facts are the facts and so there is no change of them. What do the old facts mean? Well, that changes every day. In reconsiderations of the past—especially of the unpleasant past—it is common to assume a pseudo-reflective, I-have-had-a-learning-experience posture, and then report out to the world the new person you are. I find that hollow and tedious. No one changes much, as far as I can see. Looking back now on then, those experiences then meant something then that they still mean now—that it is important to stop dishonesty and fakery. I think as a senior university administrator, you are forced into being functionally dishonest, saying empty positives in expected public academic discourse, all the while keeping the real truth of an institution—its crunches, impossibilities, and realistic sense of itself and its future—behind the villa walls. Over the course of twenty-five years, from chair to dean to president,

I found myself becoming a robotic academic apologist and increasingly disillusioned with its dishonesty. To do the job, I turned into a kind of anti-intellectual; the events that happened were a necessary part of me giving that up and getting genuine freedom, which I think I have now.

Is there any evidence that publishing the piece made it more difficult to find another academic position? Any easier?

Nothing either way. The events doomed my academic life, and I recognized that very quickly, when close friends of very high influence could not even get me an interview somewhere. But the piece allowed me to say fully and to the whole world what happened, what caused it, and what it meant at the time. I am forever grateful to the *Washington Post* for that opportunity.

You seem quite comfortable with what you are doing now, and with the journey of self-discovery you have undertaken. Is that correct?

I'm not a journey of self-discovery kind of guy. I have my next life going. The Saudi people who run the company where I work are honest, caring, generous, and sincere. They know everything about my past, as do all my staff and most everyone here, and no one gives a hoot (except the ever-lurking Luddites who use embarrassment to their own manipulative ends—I am used to these people and I now punch back). My company has been generous and supportive of me and I have been able to use my experience and knowledge to help them. We are now arguably the top education company in the Kingdom, and we have moved to this position in nine months. I owe my bosses a lot for their trust in me, and I will help them unhesitatingly. Happy? Not sure what that word means anymore. I am productive, using my brain, and I am constantly learning—from Arabic to Islam to Mideast politics and culture and history, to a new awareness of a line of influence that stretches from Rabat to Manila. In many ways my life now is so much more than I had in fifty-plus years prior.

Speaking of that line of influence from Rabat to Manila—this is the kind of thing that underscores my previous points about the dishonesty and fakery of the American university leadership persona that I am so glad to leave behind. As a dean and president, I had to spout "globalization" all the time. Global this and global that. This is a term that now seems to me either meaningless or entirely relative to the worldview of the user. There is a fifteen-century-old line of faith and business that runs straight from Morocco to the Philippines and that has drawn Muslims and workers of need to countries of religion and economic opportunity. Saudi Arabia is a classic example of a receiving country in this respect. As a consequence there are some Kerala here from India, or Malaysian Muslims, who are more globalized than well-off students from the U.S. who have had canned globalization experiences as part of their university's "twenty-first-century competencies." But no one knows about this faith-economics line or even talks about it in the U.S. Now imagine if, as a college president, I said, "This institution is going to put into public dialectic the tension of the globalization of DC- and Eurocentric individualistic capitalism and the seven-times older, community-oriented globalization of the Islamic socioeconomic line from Rabat to Manila." People would say, "What happened to Dr. Frawley? Has he gone bonkers!?" I would get a visit from the board chairman asking me just what is going on and then there would be a public announcement that Dr. Frawley has decided to (ahem) "spend more time with his family." The irony is that I could say all this as a professor, but the requisite persona of American institutional leadership prevents me from saying it as a president, and instead forces upon me a bland fakeness. In short, I can speak the truth as a professor but am increasingly prevented from speaking the truth as I rise in leadership positions. Not until we free our university leaders from this kind of thought-discourse straightjacket and dishonesty will we advance Western education in any substantive sense of the word "advance."

Do you think the board would have behaved the same way had you been in office more than a year?

Unlikely. I think the board had to do what it really did not want to do, and it would have done so no matter what the time frame. Many members of the board wanted to figure out a way for me to stay—in some form—and they told me so. And the hundreds of supportive letters and e-mails I received from the public further ratified that view. But pressure from the region (including major donors and political figures) and pressure from the Virginia public education system made the board's decision for them. There is a kind of Old Testament God to Virginia public life—the God who throws lightning at transgressors. I think that, perhaps because of inexperience, the board didn't know what it could do and found itself as a body with ultimatums it could not control, even though the board itself consisted of smart and reasonable people who believed in dialogue over retribution. So they voted unanimously in public, but split and argued in private. And here we come back to the honesty lesson, whose knife cuts all ways, not just on me.

Did your contract have insufficient safeguards against arbitrary board action?

What would you advise selectees to include in their contracts to prevent what happened to you from happening to them?

To this day, I recall the words of my brother, an influential lawyer in the NY-NJ area:

"Remember, there is no such thing as a contract." Said by a lawyer, such observations stand you up quickly. A board can do anything, really, and claim motivation (as can any contractor—come to Saudi!), and protections have an assurance role more than anything with teeth and substance. I think my contract was fine. All safeguards seem to me to work as part of the threatening background. Did Penn State's president's have a Joe Paterno clause in it?

Was the board unanimous throughout the ordeal? Were there people who supported you and tried to at least negotiate a reasonable severance and continued professorial tenure?

Officially? Of course. Really? No. Board members told me privately of their desires, as I tried to point out previously. But the currently unavoidable gap between public and private in university higher administration (part of the functional dishonesty I described above) makes for apparent unanimity.

Politics and the President

MICHAEL GARRISON, WEST VIRGINIA UNIVERSITY
(2007–2008)

Founded in 1867, West Virginia University (WVU) is a large, public research university with nearly 30,000 students at its main campus in Morgantown, West Virginia, and at four divisional campuses around the state. It is governed by the WVU Board of Governors and the West Virginia Higher Education Policy Commission. Michael Garrison's appointment as president was controversial from the time his candidacy became known. He had been managing member of Spilman Thomas & Battle law firm in Morgantown. He had also served as chief of staff for former governor Bob Wise and as cabinet secretary in the West Virginia Department of Tax and Revenue.

During his brief tenure as president, Garrison pushed through the biggest raises for faculty and staff members in fifteen years. He landed a $25-million donation, the largest private gift in the university's history. He led the charge for an expensive public-private program to pay for research and faculty recruitment, and externally funded research increased by 7 percent. But, Garrison also bucked the culture when he pressed a lawsuit for contract abrogation against a beloved football coach who had fled to greener pastures. In

2008, Garrison became embroiled in a scandal involving the granting of an executive masters of business administration (EMBA) degree to the governor's daughter, who had failed to complete the required credits.

Garrison's departure from the presidency exemplifies several interlocking derailment themes. The institutional context is primary. Garrison's appointment was opposed by the faculty from the outset because he was not an academic. One might argue that Garrison failed to comprehend the depth of feeling in the community and among the alumni about the decision to sue the departed football coach for failing to live up to the terms of his contract. The subsequent and very public controversy over whether or not the former governor's daughter had completed the requirements for an earned EMBA degree added fuel to the fire. The board's unpredictable vacillations over the issue of the degree combined with the original antagonism on campus to doom his presidency.

The Search

In 2006, the Board of Governors at West Virginia University (WVU) announced that the president since 1995 would be leaving. When the search consultant called to tell me that I had been nominated, I was flattered but not completely surprised. I had been approached by friends and colleagues interested in nominating me. At the time, I was a partner in a large law firm, had served as chief of staff to Governor Bob Wise of West Virginia, and was the chairman of the state's Higher Education Policy Commission. I was an untraditional presidential candidate who was recruited for the job by those who stated a desire for aggressive change at the state's flagship institution.

I was one of a dozen candidates invited to airport interviews with the search committee. Clearly, the committee saw me as the outside candidate. I had far more business, legal, and government experience than other candidates, but my higher education experience was limited to my experience as a first-generation college student and student body president, service on the West Virginia Higher Education Policy Commission and as an adjunct faculty member in the WVU Department of Political Science. In evaluating whether to participate in the search, however, I had determined that my candidacy would represent a distinct change from the WVU and higher education status quo and, if selected, I would offer tangible results with a more business-oriented approach to the job than that of my predecessor.

The final part of the search included a two-day on-campus interview. Student and staff forums drew large audiences and were serious but hopeful in tone. As I left the public forum, I was stopped by a woman who had been a classified staffer for forty-one years and had never been more encouraged that she might have some "say" in how the place was run if I got the job. Students liked the idea that I had been a student there myself and worked to put myself through school as a first-generation college graduate. As I reached out to first-generation students they began to reach back to discuss our shared backgrounds. The faculty forum was marked by contradictions. I was too young to handle the job, but needed "enough energy to take us to the next level." I needed to know how to navigate the state funding process to win increases in faculty salaries, but my background was "too political." I would have to be able to tackle bureaucracy and inefficiency on campus, but my business background was suspect because "a university cannot be run like a business." An emerging trend at the time, many of the faculty questions derived from anonymous blog postings that had no basis in fact.

After the open forums, I had a more detailed interview with the full board. Board members asked me to respond to the charge that I was too nontraditional, business- and change-oriented, and politically astute. Acknowledging these traits, I posed my own question in response: "Based upon your search criteria and the national data from sitting presidents as to what they believe is important for a president to be successful, isn't that the kind of president you're looking for?" To a person, the board members present agreed.

On April 13, 2007, a 15-1 vote by the board of governors elected me the twenty-second president of West Virginia University.

Transition: The First One Hundred Days

Prior to my election, the faculty senate passed a vote of no confidence in the presidential search, which had had more than one hundred applicants and took more than six months to complete. So, I began my first meeting with the executive committee of the Faculty Senate by acknowledging I was essentially a runner-up in what ultimately became a two-person race. Knowing that I had work to do, I asked for an honest assessment of their priorities and was surprised that most of them had a tough time describing an agenda at all. After subsequent meetings and my reiteration that I was committed to serious change rather than the status quo, I discovered that they were most concerned about faculty salaries, welfare, and stability, all of which had a huge impact on retention.

Despite some vocal detractors, many faculty members embraced the spirit of change and rapid progress I introduced. During the summer of 2007, a group of young faculty (some supporting me, some opposing, and some undecided) suggested a series of town-hall meetings to engage the entire campus in moving the university forward. New senior staff members embraced the concept. Those holdovers from the prior administration voiced concerns about creating a platform for my critics and critics of the university in general. When I asked the board chair to join me in hosting the forums, he essentially forbade me from moving forward with the idea because it was "too open." Trusting my instincts, we ignored this advice and invited the campus community and general public to "Join the Conversation" and hosted several thousand individuals in eight very successful public forums. Our board vice-chairman, who saw the real value in engaging the campus community, even agreed to moderate one of the forums, so the board was represented after all.

Early Traction

As the transition period ended, our focus moved from collecting data to action. When I questioned long-standing university policies and procedures that made little sense, we heard a common refrain: "that's the way we've always done it." Tradition explained why the president's cabinet meeting—known as "the 8:15 group"—convened at 8:30 without any attendance or reporting requirements. It explained why the 2001 Classified Staff Salary Schedule had not been fully funded for almost a decade and why a classified research university relied almost exclusively on the uncertainty of earmarks. It explained why the dysfunctional health sciences function had not been reviewed or revised in twenty years.

As we listened to the campus constituencies, a desire for more radical change became palpable and we worked hard to deliver. Thanks to incredible assistance from those around me, we came out of the gates strong with improvements that hit the bottom line, such as increases in the state budget, the two largest faculty and staff pay raise packages in twenty years, and reenergized private giving, including the single largest gift of $25 million to WVU. We made real commitments to social responsibility with a multimillion dollar partnership for energy efficiency and research, a green footprint project, and the "one WVU campaign" to address campus diversity. We enhanced the quality of campus life with the construction of a campus childcare center that had been studied—but never implemented—for three decades. We strengthened town-gown relations through safety improvements and new student housing.

By the end of my first one hundred days, the media had given us an "A."As we made great strides in just a few months, members of the university community with big ideas clamored to be more involved. For example, after we announced the $25-million donation, a professor who had been openly critical of me during the search sent me a lengthy e-mail of apology and praise. She now saw an opportunity in my political contacts and expressed hope in using them to find funding for her own research project.

Board members were also caught up in this wave of optimism and began to push for even more aggressive change. While some of them may have had their own agendas, for the most part, their mandate for action was well intentioned and pervasive. Within six months, however, two complicated and highly public issues proved to be more than many on our board, particularly the chairman, were capable of navigating. These issues, and how the board handled them, undermined my leadership and ultimately, derailed my presidency.

Issue #1: The Coaching Departure

In 2006, before the search for my presidency, the head football coach at WVU, Rich Rodriguez, had been engaged in a very public courtship with the University of Alabama. It ended in an impromptu press conference at which Rodriguez said, I plan "on being at West Virginia the rest of my career."

Soon after the announcement, it became clear that the prior WVU administration had asked a group of football boosters to negotiate "whatever it takes" terms to keep Rodriguez. That deal, however risky for the university, should have been memorialized in a signed contract. When I began my presidency eight months later, however, I was astounded to learn that the celebrated booster-negotiated deal still had not resulted in a signed contract. This scenario illuminated the exceptionally poor management of the relationship between the university's athletic function and its boosters prior to my presidency. No doubt, athletic boosters are important to the overall success of an athletic program, but they should not have control over operating details of a university program. Our efforts to reverse this trend were controversial as we pushed to finalize the terms of the agreement. In August 2007, we finally signed a contract with Rodriguez.

What happened next was the last thing anyone anticipated. In December, Rodriguez announced he would be leaving to coach at the University of Michigan. I learned this from a breaking news segment on ESPN. Rodriguez made it clear he was leaving because we refused to meet a list of demands that went well beyond his booster-negotiated deal. We refused, at least in part, because several of his demands would have caused major issues—internally and with the NCAA—and other universities which had done similar things were now under investigation.

Rodriguez's contract contained a $4-million buyout clause. Asked about paying the penalty at his Michigan press conference, Rodriguez answered that "the lawyers are working on it." At hearing this, we were concerned that he did not intend to honor the contract he had signed just months earlier. After meeting with WVU counsel and the board, we decided to sue Rodriguez to recover the money. We made the decision for a single reason—it was our job to protect the university.

Our decision to file the lawsuit was instantly controversial. Rather than rallying behind the university, some in the campus community (including some board members) criticized the lawsuit. Some athletic boosters attacked me for failing to concede to the coach's requests. Some fans and alumni claimed I made a bad situation worse because of the publicity. The media portrayed me as a bully for pursuing damages. Some faculty suggested I put athletics ahead of academics. The university foundation board members who were responsible for negotiating with the coach in 2006 grilled me about the situation. They were disappointed the coach was not given everything he wished. Perhaps it is a sad statement on the priorities of the public, but of all the issues I dealt with in my time as president, no other issue came close in generating such negative response.

The litigation was ultimately resolved favorably for the university that July 2008, when Rodriguez decided he would pay in full, with a little help from his new school. Suddenly, what had been cause for controversy became a reason for celebration. Board critics made an about face and suddenly supported the lawsuit. The media called it precedent setting in an area where schools are normally far outmatched by the coach's legal team. At that point, however, I had already announced my resignation.

Issue #2: An Executive MBA Degree

In October 2007, while rushing off to teach my political science class, a former university student called me. She had just received a promotion at a large pharmaceutical company and press releases included that she had earned an executive MBA (EMBA) from WVU. When reporters called the university to verify this degree, Admissions and Records was unable to do so. She was irate at this response and adamant that she had earned the degree based in part on credits granted for work experience.

The only conversation I ever had with the student regarding her claim, lasted less than five minutes, and it was clear she was angry. I told her I was sorry she was upset, but—at the moment—had no way of knowing whether she had the degree or what her former program advisor had arranged with her a decade earlier (she claimed to have graduated in 1998 and did participate in the actual ceremony). I told her I would ask someone to look into it and that that person would get back to her. I had known the student casually for a number of years. We were natives of the same hometown, her company was a regular client of my law firm, and she was the daughter of the then-governor of West Virginia (not the governor for whom I had served as chief of staff).

I asked my staff to have the appropriate academic officials, including the provost, explore the facts and received their report within two weeks. The academic officials in the College of Business and Economics and provost reported that the former student had an arrangement to earn experiential credit and, based upon this arrangement, believed she possessed the degree, although there were no academic records indicating she had completed the full forty-eight credit hours required by the program. The administrators expressed concern that the record keeping in this particular program had been a problem since its creation in the mid-1990s.

In December 2007, news reports made the inquiry public. Faculty wanted a review panel to study the matter. The provost and the board chair did not. I pushed in the other direction and wanted to insure the process used by those who reviewed the situation was as transparent as possible. In the end, the decision to confirm the EMBA was scrutinized by the board, a faculty senate panel, the dean of the college, and an external, independent auditor. All but the faculty panel supported the conclusions that there was reasonable belief that the degree should be granted and that the program had seriously inadequate record-keeping protocols. The faculty panel report led to the most controversy, and, ironically, was filled with the most assumption and speculation, rather than any real empirical analysis.

To address the record-keeping issues, along with a group of staff and faculty members, we outlined a plan to implement the review panel's recommendations and to ensure the EMBA program—for the first time since it was started in the 1990s—would incorporate uniform practices for academic record keeping, experiential credit, and independent study. We also asked the American Association of Collegiate Registrars and Admission Officers (AACRAO) to audit our academic record-keeping practices across the university to determine if there were indeed serious flaws.

In early 2009, after I departed the university, the AACRAO report concluded that the EMBA program failed to articulate and follow records retention standards, had an inconsistent practice of recording transfer credits on official transcripts, and lacked a definition for applying experiential credit toward degrees in the College of Business and Economics. AACRAO also determined that an unusually large number of previous EMBA degrees were "flawed" in the sense that they did not reflect the required number of credit hours for graduation—just like the case of the former student whose inquiry caused the audit in the first place. Although the independent AACRAO report confirmed what the academic officials discovered in October 2007, the interim administration of university officials in 2009 failed to provide any meaningful explanation for the various other deficient degrees and no explanation has been provided to the public to date.

A Shift in Board Practices

In the aftermath of the EMBA issue, most of the board was in disarray. The chair and other board members, who had initially railed against the review panel, changed their position when the negative findings were released—even though they privately acknowledged the complete lack of empirical analysis performed by the panel. A handful of board members called emergency meetings, and the chair, who was becoming far more concerned with public opinion and his chairmanship, convened an ad hoc subcommittee without telling other board members or me. On the morning of April 23, 2008, I was informed by voicemail of a board meeting scheduled for that afternoon.

When I arrived at the meeting, it was clear that many board members had not been informed why the meeting was called. The chair called the meeting to order and immediately took the board into executive session, where there was minimal opportunity for any real analysis of the panel report. Afterward, a formal charge from the board chair included the following statement: "It is the recommendation of the Board that you as President of West Virginia University accept responsibility for errors in judgment and procedures relative to this matter made by members of, and personnel affiliated with, the Administration." While the chair exempted me from any blame, I was specifically charged with reviewing the report and personnel involved and with developing plans and policies to prevent such situations from happening again. I was to report back to the board at its regularly scheduled meeting on June 6, 2008. After the meeting, a clearly hostile board chair explained that even though the board approved of my handling of the situation, he and certain board members "were just sick and tired of this issue and reading about the board in the paper" and that I was going to have to "fix it."

I set about addressing the issue. I met with academic officials to gather information about how the decision was made. The dean confirmed that he made the ultimate decision in consultation with his colleagues. Upon learning this, I expressed my anger to the provost that the academic officials allowed the transcripts to be modified when the dean could have waived the credit requirements, and I asked the provost to ask the dean to step down as a result. When the provost resisted, I explained he would need to step down as well if he did not reprimand the dean. On April 28, 2008, both the dean and provost resigned.

In early May, I received a vote of "no confidence" from the faculty senate despite the fact that no one could identify exactly what I had done wrong. The board chair's ad hoc subcommittee continued to meet, often without me or my staff. The board held a three-hour emergency meeting to discuss the negative publicity without notifying anyone in the administration. The meeting, to which I was not invited, coincided with a statement from the governor in which he expressed his conflicted feeling as a father and as governor, stated confidence in me, but affirmed the board's ultimate authority in deciding how to handle the situation. He was clearly overwhelmed by the media swarm and attempting to distance himself from the situation. Ironically, once the media began writing about the inquiry earlier in the year, the governor called me to ask why I failed to discuss this issue to him back in October 2007. "Governor," I replied, "I had absolutely no reason to inform you and just about every reason not to."

Because I felt that we had met its charge a week early, I asked the board to convene a meeting on May 30 so that I could present my findings and plan. In the executive session, I asked each board member to tell me directly if he or she continued to support me or wished for me to resign. Although they said they supported me, several wondered aloud why we were "trying to do so much so fast"—a far cry from their earlier support of our change agenda. After the meeting, the board issued a statement: "It's important to note that the Board believes that there is no evidence whatsoever that President Garrison took any action to improperly influence the grant of an EMBA degree. The Board will continue to review all appropriate matters, meet again on June 6 and will have further comment at that time."

Decision to Step Down

After the May meeting, I tried to return to the important work of executing our plans for the university. Had the board been equipped to stand together and move forward, we might have succeeded. While some board members shared this philosophy, most were still sensitive to public pressure. Wanting a symbolic head on a platter, several board members, including the chair, encouraged me to fire someone, such as my chief of staff or general counsel. While willing to listen to the board, I was not willing to take an unwarranted action and refused to do so. Other board members explained that they were pressured by a public letter calling for my dismissal—ignoring the fact that the letter was penned by two boosters who were personal friends of the departed football coach and another who campaigned openly to be given the job of president during my search.

I believed that standing firm in the face of the media firestorm would allow the legitimate facts to emerge. Many on the board, however, became analytically weak when it came to dealing with unsubstantiated media stories; this reaction only granted such commentary increasing influence over their actions. Especially when an institution is under attack, its board and a president need to stand united. However, by the regularly scheduled June meeting, a mere week after the board expressed support, I knew I could no longer count on support from the entire board. At the end of my report to the board, which included our record faculty and staff pay increases and the results of a successful legislative session, I announced that I would step down as president. I explained that I was honored to serve a school I deeply loved, that I was extremely proud of our progress, and that I knew we needed to continue our aggressive change agenda. But, the public discussion had become far too focused on me, to the detriment of the university.

Much like the public controversy, the board was ill-prepared to handle my departure. Without discussing it with me, the board chair publicly suggested I could serve as a consultant to the university or even an advisor to the board.

Asked by a reporter if this might create a backlash, he replied "there will be backlash if we don't shoot him." The board chair and the ad hoc subcommittee had been so consumed with handling the negative press that they hadn't figured out how to handle the two years left on my contract. While fellow attorneys encouraged me to demand my contract be honored by filing a lawsuit, I had no interest in doing so, particularly if it meant continued interactions with hand-wringing board members concerned only with their own public perception. A few of them approached me privately about a severance package, but that was the least of my concerns and never why I took the job in the first place.

Those few short months of discord drained the spirit of change and energy from the university and the enthusiasm for still-needed change was replaced by a call for stability and status quo. In the wake of my resignation, WVU lost some highly skilled staff and some board members, who were supportive in both private and public, refused reappointment.

Epilogue

It is ironic that I was recruited by the board as a business-oriented candidate who was charged to produce tangible results based on facts and empirical data; however, my departure was precipitated by members of my board running from rumors on blogs and afraid of their own personal press clippings. Perhaps I should have foreseen that for many in the university community and board, there was never really an interest in true change for the institution. This is foreshadowed by recalling the advice I received from a major university donor (who is now, not surprisingly, a member of the governing board) to make few really big or controversial decisions in the first three years of my presidency because "things at a university move slowly enough that by the time your first contract is up, you can renegotiate a longer one and save really controversial decisions until then." The reasoning behind this thinking is not unlike the advice given to political candidates today who are told that getting elected (and reelected) and solving problems are most often mutually exclusive things.

Despite these admonitions, however, the list that the staffer and donor would have rather seen put off became the framework for my official list of goals and objectives as submitted to my board during my first year as president. Just a year after putting the list together, in the summer of 2008, one of my last duties as president was to participate in a performance review of the past year. During this review, the board determined that our administration had met and exceeded all of our listed goals and objectives—we had essentially completed in one year an agenda that was projected to cover several years by the traditional higher education administration standard.

The board members present for this review were clearly conflicted in their observations. On the one hand, they were all quite pleased to join in the celebration of the largest faculty and staff pay raises and one-time private contribution in the history of our university (not to mention the successful culmination of the lawsuit against our former coach—making the athletic department 4 million dollars richer). On the other hand, they admitted that they were not prepared for the way our aggressive agenda for change would take them and many others out of their comfort zone. Although the board made one last attempt to arrange for me to serve as a consultant to work to continue many of the changes we had started, I had no confidence at that point that they had a sincere interest in moving our change agenda forward and declined the proposal. It was also clear that the plan to bring an interim president on board was an even louder signal to return to the status quo.

Even with just a year to work with, it is easy to see now, a few years later, the ripple effects that true change, if allowed even for a short period of time, can bring to a campus. Things that have happened since our administration— like the announcement of a new student health complex, public forums being held to discuss a campus master plan, and the beginnings of a structural change in health sciences—all have their roots in our year of hard work and push for long-needed change.

Hindsight: What Can We Learn from Derailed Presidents?

As demonstrated by Frawley's and Garrison's accounts, derailment can and does occur whether or not the incumbent is meeting the academic and financial expectations of the board. These two presidents made positive contributions to their universities. They both enjoyed at least some measure of constituent support. For Garrison, lingering resentment about his appointment played a role in his derailment, as did the board's shifting responses to publicity about the events described.

But, these two accounts serve as reminders that college and university presidents live under the glare of the media spotlight. Ethical lapses—real or perceived—are likely to derail college and university presidents, not to mention elected officials and military leaders. The ubiquity of media (social and otherwise) and diminishing privacy make personal crises more likely to be discovered and broadcast, in turn increasing the potential for derailment.

In Frawley's case, the personal crisis that ended his tenure was not primarily ethical in nature. Furthermore, it is not at all clear that more effective scrutiny of his personal life prior to this presidency would have revealed that the pressures of the job and his decision not to move his family to Virginia would culminate in a series of unfortunate choices.

Garrison's essay is not intended to help a reader decide whether Garrison was guilty of any lapse in judgment. These essays are valuable because they represent firsthand accounts not often disclosed because of confidentiality agreements.

Presidencies of public institutions may be more fraught than those in the independent sector with politics and publicity. Appointed and elected boards often have dual loyalties—to the institution and to those who appointed or elected them. Some bring strong political opinions about public higher education to their duties as board members and attempt to use their influence to direct curricular and research priorities. Dysfunctional independent sector boards exist as well (see chapter 2). In all cases, public airing of laundry—clean or dirty—is anathema.

More casus lead to belli these days than in the past. But should they? In the criminal and civil justice systems, a range of sanctions is available to those responsible for recommending what action to take for each transgression and in each case. Belief in redemption, belief in the efficacy of counseling and coaching, belief in board development is exhibited by presidents and boards every day. In the context of a book on presidential derailments, questions worth considering include: Would the outcome have been the same if these two presidents had been in their fifth year rather than their first? Might a track record of accomplishment have led the boards to be more tolerant and more lenient? Does the derailment reflect poorly on the board's choice of a president or the processes that led to it? Or does the derailment reflect the crucible in which every president in higher education is tested?

Some derailed presidents have recovered well. Evan Dobelle has had five successful presidencies, though he was derailed by political machinations in Hawaii. Robert A. Hoover left the University of Idaho under a cloud because of financial mismanagement of a major project, but he enjoyed a successful presidency at the College of Idaho. In presidential searches, a previous derailment is not necessarily a disqualifier. As so often in life, circumstances alter cases. Trying to generalize lessons from any given derailment is less important than making efforts to improve executive searches, leadership transitions, board practices and behaviors, and board-president relations. However, in the next few chapters, we look at how the aggregate of institutions we have studied—and our own experiences in the field of higher education—point to some ways that boards and presidents can minimize derailments in the future.

PART II / Averting the Train Wreck

The Upstream Solution

More Thoughtful Academic Searches

Too often, the only candidate that can survive such a scrutiny process is the one who is least provocative. No one involved in the scrutiny process may have been particularly pleased, but no one was especially offended either. And several years may go by before those involved in the scrutiny process awaken to the fact that bland, noncommittal leadership is not what the times require.

STEPHEN JOEL TRACHTENBERG, "NOT WHAT IT'S CRACKED UP TO BE"

The Imprecision of Presidential Searches

Some presidential searches are run well and produce long-serving and high-performing leaders. Too often, however, it is a matter of luck rather than the outcome of a sound process. When colleges, universities, and systems set out to find a new president, they often begin and end in self-delusion. They declare their intention to find the best person for the job. Then, after all the sorting and sifting, they announce that they have indeed found the best person for the job. But, in fact, they may have done no such thing. After the audition—the interrogations, the checking, the interviews, and the hazing—they have no way of knowing how good the last woman or man left standing will really be. The institution only learns that much later.

A more reasonable approach would be for us to seek and then announce that we have found a very good person, an excellent fit for the institution, and a president of wonderful potential. That does not constitute hedging the bets, but it is entirely forthcoming. Honesty would also compel us to say that we believe we have found the best person available to us. Of course, no one wants to say this, but everyone should. Often, the selectee is a second choice for one reason or another—a spouse did not like the idea of living in Manhattan, New York, or Manhattan, Kansas, or the "best" candidate turned down the job. In reality, the institution ends up with the best candidate who is available and willing. Many second choices perform splendidly. In the end, search committees and boards chose well, and they were lucky.

Luck is not the product of reason or of academic acuity. Given the process by which new leaders in the academy are chosen, getting the best person available may be happenstance. Why? First, a candidate's curriculum vita is a tombstone of past accomplishments, but the client is looking toward a different institution's future. As advertisements for investment firms often state, "past performance is no guarantee of future returns." Second, rising rank in organizational hierarchies and a list of eminent publications do not reveal how the candidate will go about fundraising, making peace between warring factions of the faculty, or dealing with drunken students and angry parents. Even a candidate who has had experience as a senior administrator has been in charge of executing policy, not creating it, and—equally important—deciding when not to create it.

Candidates need to ask themselves whether they are interested in a presidency for the right reasons. Do they aspire to a presidency because they perceive it as a position that will enhance their earnings and perquisites? Are they prepared for the demands a presidency makes on family life and privacy? Are they temperamentally suited to shared governance and compromise and the generally slow pace of academic decision making? Are they financially stable enough to risk failure or derailment without irreparably damaging their futures? Do they understand the importance of having an attorney experienced in writing presidential contracts to negotiate on their behalf with members of the board?

None of this is a cause for melancholy. A presidency at a successful institution will always attract strong applicants. Even less successful institutions are likely to attract people who are drawn to the challenge. Talent is available.

Suggestions for a Successful Search

To find that talent, the institution—especially the search committee and the board—must work collaboratively to develop a frank assessment of the institution's conditions and aspirations, its financial circumstances, its opportunities and challenges. They ought to prioritize the qualities and characteristics important to future success. They must consider what experience is necessary and what is merely desirable. They must think hard about insisting on (or rejecting) someone who has been a president or a faculty member or has significant private sector or government experience.

The following seven suggestions are designed to cope with the unpredictability of circumstances and the vagaries of human nature, to reduce the chances and instances of derailment, and to enable successful presidential searches:

1. Undertake a governing board assessment
2. Be selective in appointing the search committee
3. Clarify what, if any, professional guidance and support are needed
4. Prioritize characteristics of the next president
5. Share information and establish mutual expectations
6. Screen candidates with care
7. Speak with one voice about the appointment

These suggestions have been alluded to in earlier chapters. Collecting them here reveals their interaction, and synthesizing them is intended to help institutional and community stakeholders during the formative stages of any presidential search.

In every case, boards and search committees must temper their role as institutional advocates with candor about institutional challenges. The board must not fail to disclose information about the financial and other problems the college, university, or system faces. They should also expect that candidates can and should undertake their own due diligence.

Undertake a Governing Board Assessment

The departure of a president, regardless of the combination of reasons, is a natural opportunity to pause, reflect, and assess the operations of the governing board. In many instances, the board will attempt to ascertain the characteristics and skills most needed in the next president, but it often fails to evaluate its own structure, operations, and performance as part of the institutional leadership structure.

As revealed in the case studies, diminished board functionality is a frequent theme in presidential derailments. Boards have been known to fall prey to dysfunctional group dynamics and political machinations. The board at Dogwood Community College had little turnover and less appetite for confrontation with faculty. When Daniel tried to revise faculty job descriptions, he antagonized the faculty. The board caved to a faculty vote of no confidence, and Daniel left shortly thereafter (see chapter 5). Boards have also been known to have their own ethical lapses, most frequently conflicts of interest. Because they were one and the same person, Carol at Caroline College was never certain whether she was getting expert advice from legal counsel or a suggestion from the board chair (see chapter 2).

A governing board assessment conducted prior to a presidential search can assure board members, as well as presidential candidates, that the board is functioning ethically and effectively. The board itself may be a factor in a candidate's consideration of the presidency. To be most valuable to the institution, a board assessment should be conducted by an independent consultant and should include both qualitative and quantitative approaches so that it generates a full picture of board performance. A comprehensive board assessment looks at the more technical issues of compliance (policies and procedures) and structure (committees and meetings), as well as the softer issues of group dynamics and board engagement. The board self-assessment process may include interviews or a survey. It should be anonymous so that individuals feel comfortable speaking candidly, and the resulting reports should remain confidential within the board. If the governance assessment leads to recommendations, changes to board policies and procedures can be made prior to the selection of a new president.

Be Selective in Appointing the Search Committee

Traditionally, the composition of the search committee is designed to satisfy demographic optics but not necessarily to engage adequate expertise in the complex task of hiring a president. Unlike search committees in industry, academic search committees often include faculty from a few disciplines, board members, administrators, staff, students, alumni, and neighbors. Campus representation is broad, but understanding of the presidential task is narrow. Committee members each strive to select the individual most likely to advance their stakeholder group's interests, often overlooking a more comprehensive, holistic view of the enterprise.

Search committee members are earnest and put in long hours evaluating candidates on paper and in person. Most likely, they have never done anything like this before and are unlikely ever to do it again. Productive search committees are small and comprised of individuals with experience in senior level hiring decisions. Presidential searches are daunting, especially for board members with limited experience in higher education and human resources, not to mention time and resource constraints. Those creating search teams should tap board members who have experience with executive level personnel decisions in their professional lives to work with the search committee and serve as a liaison to the full board. Faculty and staff members should be selected from those who have demonstrably served the institution well and helped fill other leadership positions in the institution.

The search committee should not be designed to provide a voice for every stakeholder. Instead, it should make sure that the search process is inclusive and allows ample opportunity for input from multiple constituencies. Students have minimal experience in searches, limited appreciation of the academy's culture, and (unlike other search committee members) no fiduciary responsibilities. Search committees ought to listen to student leaders and pay close attention to their perspective, but they ought not to grant them voting membership on the committee.

CLARIFY WHAT, IF ANY, PROFESSIONAL GUIDANCE AND SUPPORT ARE NEEDED

Whether to work with a search firm is a consequential decision, as is how much assistance is required. A competent search firm can assist a board and a search committee in undertaking a thoughtful process for finding the next president. But, it comes with clear financial costs and some less tangible trade-offs. Board and search committee members must determine what they can undertake themselves and what kind of guidance and support they need.

A competent search firm can be of enormous assistance. Armed with the right experience in higher education and expertise gleaned from managing countless searches, search firms can cast wider nets more quickly and streamline the process. This takes the burden off of board and staff members at the institution who have their regular jobs to do. Of course, this costs money. For the institution, the expenses are not insignificant, and they may not have been anticipated.

Search firms have, at their disposal, a wide variety of instruments for evaluating whether a candidate has the agreed-upon qualities; it is far more common in industry than in academe for the search committee to prioritize a list of qualities, attributes, and skills. Academics, by and large, may distrust these instruments, sensing a whiff of the social sciences when what they want is humanism, even though the two categories are artificial (Lubker 2011).

The decision to hire a search firm should be driven by institutional circumstances and board expertise. Institutions that have not undertaken a presidential search in recent memory may need more services and support from a search firm. Those who have recently undertaken serious institutional analyses of their programs and administrative functioning may need less help.

Generally speaking, search firm fees do not vary dramatically, and their guarantees against a derailment are similar. But, the search committee needs to find the right firm. Soliciting several proposals helps ensure that the board and institution find a good fit. The search committee should interview the individual who would be assigned to their search, not just principals in the firm. It should consider asking questions such as:

- Does the firm have a track record of success with similar institutions?
- How does the firm ensure diversity throughout the process?
- What is the firm's record of failures (quickly derailed presidents), as well as successes?
- What differentiates the firm's searches from those of other companies? Are they more skilled in helping the institution define priorities? In crafting specific job descriptions? In bringing forward large numbers of well-qualified candidates? In conducting background investigations? In offering on-boarding assistance to the board and new president?
- How many other searches will the consultants assigned to the institution be responsible for during the duration of the search?

Prioritize Characteristics of the Next President

Distinguishing one college, university, or system president advertisement from another is difficult because each describes an ideal of personal qualities and experience rather than a human being with strengths and weaknesses.

Likewise, the institutions are all presented as strong and vibrant, rising in the national rankings and on the verge of becoming the Harvard of their genus.

Too often, job descriptions are generic, rather than specific. Institutions should compose a job description that is not only accurate and complete but that also reflects institutional realities and aspirations. Search committees, governing boards, and legislators must prioritize the personal and professional qualities sought in the next president. Those priorities must be based on input from and, ideally, consensus among the stakeholders. Each stakeholder group has a different perspective on institutional needs—academics (research versus teaching), student profile (greater access versus higher standards), management style (more participatory versus more decisive). Below is the suggestion of one anonymous board member:

> This sounds parochial, but it seems to me that it would be a blessing if the University hired from within, or at least from among, the armies of talented people in and around [State] who ARE committed to this place and probably have the skill set to succeed. If part of what's needed at the University is political savvy, then maybe [retiring politician] would like something close to home to do?

There's more to hiring a president than meets the eye. Searches may get sidetracked by well-meaning board members. Making a hasty decision (or assumption) about the new president's experience and background can have the unintended effect of eliminating from the candidate pool interested and interesting people. To ensure that the best candidate available is identified, the entire board, not just the search committee, should participate in the wider discussions about institutional priorities and the kinds of candidates to be sought. The entire board has a role to play in the process and in the decision. If not informed and involved, board members may be less than fully committed to the individual ultimately selected, and some may work to undermine the presidency.

Without consensus around essential and desirable characteristics, the search will lack focus. Search committees and boards need to establish a sense of priorities. What personal characteristics are critical? What traits are nice to have? Is a terminal degree essential or desirable? Is past presidential experience a prerequisite or a bonus? Is a track record of success in fundraising mandatory? Does personality trump experience? That's not to say that searches for presidents should be mechanical. Rather, they are learning opportunities for the stakeholders as well as the candidates. A strong candidate may enlarge the initial circumference of thinking no matter how well the circle was drawn.

While the process of prioritizing candidate requirements is valuable, resist the urge to decide issues that need not be decided prior to reviewing a large number of applicants and meeting several of them. Presidential searches are an inexact art, and too many preconceived expectations can be detrimental to the process. Search committees often benefit from considering a few unconventional candidates and usually gain some deeper insights about their expectations of the president. However, if—despite the success of presidents whose experiences were as provost, corporate executive, or government leader—academic credentials are an absolute prerequisite, make that clear from the outset.

While the path to the presidency is not unimportant, the values, understandings, qualities, and skills that an individual brings to the position may be more important than for previous positions. Curiosity, compassion, and courage should be part of the equation. Personal flaws—arrogance and aloofness, condescension and controlling, dismissive and distrustful—dominate the derailment case studies. A new president must be able to build constructive relationships up, down, and to the side. As shown in the case studies, a failure in any direction often leads to a failure in office.

The more information a search committee can harvest about a candidate's interpersonal skills, the better. While difficult to deduce, conclusions about a candidate's leadership style should be based on direct questions of the individual, discreet but probing inquiries of colleagues, and sophisticated interview exercises that help surface these deep-rooted personal qualities. Ultimately, the search committee and board must determine whether the candidate's temperament, communication skills, and management style are well-suited to the culture and context of the institution. A formal or informal visit to the campuses of the finalists should be considered, and the committee should study the publically available records of their performance as well.

SHARE INFORMATION AND ESTABLISH MUTUAL EXPECTATIONS

Ignorance of the "business" of the university often results in searches without
real knowledge of the skill set and talents that are needed for leadership.
JONATHAN COLE, FORMER PROVOST OF COLUMBIA UNIVERSITY

Derailments often occur because of unresolved issues or unexplored expectations prior to employment offers and acceptances, the most common being the role of the president's spouse, the financial and overall status of the institution, and the expectations on both sides of the role of the president. The board must make certain that it clearly communicates, and that the candidate fully accepts, the core functions of the president at this particular institution—academic leader, skilled administrator, fundraiser, fence mender, turnaround expert, team builder. In institutions that are part of larger systems of higher education, boards and candidates must understand the tension between being a team player as a subordinate in a system and being a president whose primary role is institutional champion.

In order to avoid some of the misunderstandings documented in chapters 2 through 5, boards and presidents also need a common understanding of the boundaries of their respective responsibilities. For example, at Alpine Community College, board members were directly involved in making administrative decisions, such as awarding construction contracts and selecting deans. Antonio's efforts to exert his executive authority created conflicts with board members that contributed to his derailment (see chapter 5).

While boards provide overall strategic direction, presidents are integral to developing the strategic direction and almost wholly responsible for its execution. Likewise, the board has a core responsibility for fiduciary and policy oversight, but the president is also involved in establishing the oversight measures and then regularly reports to the board on progress and results. The boundaries between the responsibilities of the board and president may be defined generally, but they need to be revisited and often refined upon the arrival of a new president.

The board should articulate its expectations of the president in terms of social commitments and community involvement. The presidency is not a 9-to-5 position and needs and deserves to have some boundaries protecting his or her personal life. This is especially complicated for a college or university president, and the position often entails some accommodations for spouses and partners. Candidates should disclose any special family needs, such as a spouse who requires a university position or a desire to commute on weekends to a former residence (e.g., where a partner has other employment). The board should also establish clear policies about membership on other boards (e.g., time commitment, acceptable remuneration).

At an appropriate point early in a new president's tenure, the board and president should also agree upon a written set of performance metrics and a process for annual performance reviews (see chapter 8). This is only one aspect of the give-and-take between a president and the board. Regular communication and two-way feedback between the president and board leadership (especially the chair) will smooth out any rough edges since no document, no matter how well crafted, can anticipate every crisis or opportunity.

Screen Candidates with Care

The process of winnowing candidates through the phases of broad search, screening, and final selection is by no means objective or wholly rational. Through advertising, collegial recommendations, self-nomination, and active recruitment, a pool of a hundred candidates materializes. Fifty of them had no business applying or being recommended. Then what? The remaining candidates must be racked and stacked in some way.

Cautions for Winnowing the Candidate Pool

In their eagerness to winnow the candidate pool down to truly viable presidents and a manageable size, the search committee may rush to judgments. The follow cautions are intended to capture some of the most common mistakes made:

Look beyond the candidate's institution. Boards and search committees are often blinded by the reputation of the institution where a candidate is currently employed. Just as a Fortune 200 company wants to hire someone from a Fortune 50 company, a second-tier university often wants to hire someone from a first-tier university. They believe or hope that the current job is an imprimatur and that the hiring will burnish its reputation. The college, university, or system is hiring the person, not the previous employer.

Dig around the grapevine. Malicious gossip can ruin an otherwise sterling candidate's chances of being selected. A member of the search committee will hear from a friend who works on the same campus that the candidate is temperamental. A disgruntled faculty member at the candidate's current institution writes a letter to the search committee that contains allegations rather than facts. That hearsay could sink the applicant's chances, not just because it was unsubstantiated but, worse, because no one cared to substantiate it. Input from the candidate's home campus should be taken with a healthy dose of skepticism to ensure that personal grievances do not overtake facts. During a presidential search, judgments based on gossip should be abjured. But, rumor and hearsay should not be ignored. Claims must be investigated, not accepted, as part of whittling down a list.

Be realistic about procedural requirements. During the screening phase, it is not uncommon to find a bucket of excuses for dismissing plausible candidates. Consider these examples. A committee member points out that a candidate with admirable credentials failed to submit a list of publications. No matter that the candidate is a chemist and no one on the committee could reasonably judge the scholarship.

Beware of "group think." A special bonding takes place among committee members because of the importance and urgency of the task at hand. Their attitude, understandable and, at times admirable, is "We are doing this together and we want to be collegial, so it is better to accept easy excuses than to provoke an argument." Bonding trumps reason and equity. It also narrows the pool of finalists without the expenditure of real time or effort.

Use special care when reviewing internal candidates. Internal candidates for presidencies should be welcomed, but such candidacies bring with them the need for great sensitivity on the part of the search committee and the board.

The first decision to be made is embodied in our earlier discussion of institutional needs—what sort of leader is required at this point in the institution's history. Internal candidates who meet the criteria and priorities the board has established deserve consideration, but not every internal candidate—or perhaps any—will possess the requisite leadership style and qualities. Ensuring continuity does not require an internal candidate any more than the ability to identify and foster needed change demands a person from outside the institution.

Internal candidates may have sterling qualifications, among them an intimate knowledge of the institution's values, culture, and history. They bring a record that enjoys the trust and confidence of those within. But every internal candidate has a history at the institution. If candidates have held previous administrative positions, they will likely have made decisions that, however necessary, selected one individual or one option from a plethora of good choices—and very few poor alternatives. While those whose proposals were chosen are likely to be grateful, those associated with options not selected are likely to bear some resentment. This simply means that no internal candidate will receive unanimous acclaim. It is also more likely that gossip and rumor and personal agendas will rise to the attention of the committee and the board.

Determining how much credibility to give each negative assertion, whether and how to determine validity, is both daunting and delicate. Boards considering internal candidates must avoid any clumsiness and make extra efforts to ensure the confidentiality of their inquiries.

Undertake Thorough Background Checks

When a reasonably sized pool of candidates has been selected, say a dozen, the search committee will look at a dossier. This confidential, internal report aggregates opinions and includes a cursory credit and law enforcement check, but does little to separate fact from fiction when presenting the views of colleagues and co-workers. To be sure, that's not an easy task. It may be difficult to determine whether judgments provided are based on personal grievances or loyalties (the losing institution may be delighted to see the individual promoted away, and thus fail to be candid in discussing a candidate's personal qualities).

During the screening process, the search committee must ensure that the candidates' backgrounds and prior performances are exhaustively researched. A seemingly successful sitting president may have a hidden flaw. A previously derailed president may be perceived as tarnished goods, though some have succeeded brilliantly in subsequent presidencies. Because the reasons behind terminations are almost always subject to confidentiality agreements, the search committee may find it difficult to thoroughly investigate the circumstances.

Could the search processes at Seaside College (chapter 2) and Cypress Community College (chapter 5) have discovered that Samuel and Calvin were prone to fits of anger? Search committees should not shy away from diligent investigations that are designed to reveal hidden truths. Some of those truths may involve prior behavior, such as a history of alcohol abuse; some may indicate that a candidate has not told the whole truth about his or her personal circumstances, such as a spouse who expects a tenured position.

Boards and search committees must charge the search firm or individual committee members with making certain due diligence is undertaken. This process, though expensive, should be accomplished before the dozen candidates are whittled down to three or four finalists and prior to off-campus interviews. If not, the final list of candidates may include prospects that are in some way tarnished goods and leave the institution with fewer choices.

Look beyond the Public Persona

Presidential candidates are often interviewed seriatim or as a group by members of a search committee. They may give a presentation or several presentations to different campus constituencies. Whatever the permutation, the result is rather formal and fairly brief. Both the committee and the candidate are on dating behavior—no one wants to make a bad impression.

If the board and the president work collaboratively to identify and overcome any perceived deficiencies in performance, the president is likely to grow from strength to strength and board satisfaction will be based on sound judgment rather than the pressure to refrain from private or even public dissent. In practice, this involves a thoughtful performance evaluation process (see chapter 8).

Speak with One Voice about the Appointment

When the board reaches agreement on a candidate, it is important that the decision appear unanimous, unqualified, and enthusiastic. In practice, board members who favored other candidates feel constrained to put aside their doubts and join the chorus of praise. This is not a bad thing for the institution or the president. It demonstrates confidence and commitment to the institution's various stakeholders. To do anything less would tear the institutional fabric, as happened to Howard, who never had unified board support at the University of South Hogan. The board had been split on whether to hire Howard, and they followed the lead of an influential board member who lobbied for his appointment (see chapter 3).

Conclusion: What Not to Do

This chapter contains detailed advice about processes and procedures, and anyone who has been on either side of a search committee can add more texture to these seven recommendations. It emphasizes the interactions among search committees and boards. In the end, boards make the decision, and they would be wise to heed the warnings listed in Table 7.1. These warnings

Table 7.1.   Pitfalls of presidential searches

A board cannot expect a successful search if

- It plays politics with the search process—playing favorites, advantaging some candidates over others, letting a small group of the board manage the process.
- It is not ethical in the way the search process is designed and implemented. If the views or opinions of a few members are foisted on the board as a whole, or political judgment dictates choices, or any sort of cronyism is tolerated, these ethical failures will undermine the credibility of both the board and the president.
- It does not provide for meaningful voice and input from campus constituencies.
- It does not acquire specific and diverse evidence on how the candidate relates to a wide range of stakeholders (board members, faculty, alumni, financial benefactors, students).
- It does not insure a thorough background check on candidates' credit history.
- It does not obtain more than casual evidence of the ethics and values of the candidate.
- It does not obtain evidence on candidates' managerial traits and ability to adapt leadership style to policy, people, and place.
- It does not obtain evidence of the institutional culture perceived to exist in previous candidate assignments.
- It does not specify the leadership priorities and role expectations for the candidate.
- It is not forthcoming with the candidate on the institution's financial footing, core strengths, and operating challenges.

all center on the board because selecting the president is, arguably, the single most important responsibility of the board. Why should we be surprised with a derailment if a board has not been ethical, transparent, and careful in the search process?

Nothing here is complex or hard to grasp, and still it is a tall order. Members of the search committee and the board need to shed the Panglossian notion that they will find the best of all presidents for their institution, which is undoubtedly described as best in class. Probably they won't, and probably they aren't. Once free of that pair of delusions and with a more rational process in hand, the work of finding a new president should flow more smoothly and with greater mental comfort for everyone involved if only because unreasonable expectations of perfection arising from a necessarily imperfect activity can be put aside.

Chapter Eight

Board Dynamics

A Piece of the Presidential Derailment Puzzle

The Buck Starts and Stops with the Board

The subject of governance came up. If I can characterize it, I would say our take on the situation is that good and effective boards are a rarity and getting harder as the supply of people committed to these communities and with the influence, affluence, and wisdom needed to add value declines. . . . Why boards can't do the main thing they are most responsible for doing, which is hiring or firing presidents and directors?

BOARD MEMBER

The coerced resignation and the subsequent reinstatement of Teresa Sullivan as the president of the University of Virginia in the summer of 2012 offer a case study of a dysfunctional board.

By all media accounts (which remain unrefuted), the board chair (rector) of the board communicated her concerns about the president one at a time to a few board members. When she had a majority of votes to replace the president, she called an emergency meeting—requiring a quorum of three of sixteen members—where the agenda was terminating Sullivan's presidency.

The leadership of the board evidently believed that Sullivan was not working hard enough to lead the university in the direction and at the speed the regents wished it to take in the light of other prestigious institutions' adoption of online education in various forms. The rector developed a list of challenges facing all of higher education, not just UVA, and apparently was able to convince board members in a series of private conversations that President Sullivan had not taken sufficiently vigorous action to surmount the daunting need for change. An open question is the extent to which the president's memorandum on strategic direction had been fully debated by the board. It is not debatable that no agreed-upon performance agreement existed during Sullivan's two year tenure, and only a perfunctory review of her performance had taken place at the end of her first year. It is also plain that the board's bylaws permitted an emergency meeting when in fact there was no emergency except the imminent end of the specified term of several board members. Board members allowed themselves to be steamrolled by the chair when she announced that she had the votes to compel the end of Sullivan's presidency.

It is not at all plain that the board understood the culture of the University of Virginia, the traditions of governance in higher education, or the status and importance of the university in the public eye. While there can be no question that a variety of innovations and economic forces will compel change in higher education, each institution will adapt to the changed environment in ways consistent with its mission, resources, and responsibilities. The nation's most reputable institutions will no doubt take advantage of not just online education but also the changes in pedagogy made possible by access to online courses of distinction, and they will seek ways to make instruction more interactive and courses focused on outcomes shared within disciplinary communities. They will, like all competitive institutions both public and private, seek to enhance quality and lower costs. The pace at which our most distinguished institutions innovate will differ from each other and from institutions with missions that are less varied.

Within the space of two weeks the board's action caused the resignation of distinguished administrators and faculty members, alienated faculty, staff, students, parents, and alumni as well as legislators and the general public. It has cost the university donors and donations. It has made recruitment of faculty if not students far more difficult. The board has found it necessary to spend money to obtain public relations advice—money that could have been used for other university purposes.

President Sullivan was reinstated after the governor of Virginia stated that the board had to find a unanimous solution or be cashiered. The board met briefly (clearly after a lot of backchannel communication between its members, President Sullivan, and the governor and his representatives), and unanimously reinstated the former president. The governor then reappointed the rector and most of the board members whose terms had not expired. Evidently he charged them to work and play well together. (The events at UVA are similar to what happened to Evan Dobelle at the University of Hawaii. His experience was almost a political carbon copy except that the board, at the instigation of the governor, held an illegal meeting when he was five thousand miles away. Dobelle was let go at 10 p.m. in Honolulu. A statewide voter referendum a year later changed the constitution to alter the way university trustees were appointed.)

There's no knowing what agreement was reached with the governor, the members of the board, or President Sullivan. But it seems like the worst possible solution to keep in place both the president and her chief antagonist—the one who steamrolled other board members—and those who allowed themselves to be steamrolled. Over whose head(s) does the sword of Damocles dangle? And why? The resolution is a riddle wrapped in a mystery wrapped inside an enigma. When Churchill uttered that famous description of Russia, he stated that the key was Russian national interest. Allowing all the key players on the board to continue and the resolution of the quarrel to remain confidential will not result in the open and frank communication among the various stakeholders needed to move the university from strength to strength. It will challenge any efforts to determine an overarching institutional interest.

There's no doubt that trustees and regents have the power to hire and fire presidents, that they have a fiduciary responsibility, and that they should be focused on institutional strategy rather than tactics. But as a body (not a cabal) they should deliberate and act with sensitivity, not arrogance, with an appreciation of the institution's culture and that of higher education, with knowledge and understanding of the importance of shared governance and the necessity for an abundance of consultation and transparency. Trustees and regents share governance, though they have distinct responsibilities that no other group or actor can or should usurp.

One of any board's most important tasks is the selection of the president, the institution's or system's chief executive officer. Most of the time, they get it right (or at least good enough). But, as evidenced by the case studies, sometimes they do not. The derailment themes identified in this book recur with frequency, but the facts and circumstances of each institution are unique and multifaceted.

In every new hire, the governing board initiates the search and manages the president's arrival. In every derailment, the governing board facilitates the president's departure and negotiates its terms and conditions. Why now? Why this president? Simple answers are offered by the public relations office at the institution. The media selectively edit and sensationalize the story. But the full panoply of reasons for the derailment is unlikely to be revealed to the campus community or the public. As in most human affairs—for example, the dissolution of marriage—single motives are rare, and mixed motives common. The marriage metaphor is not chosen lightly. The emotional cost of a presidential derailment is equally weighty.

Boards do not undertake derailments without due deliberation—the costs are too high and damage to the institution's reputation inevitable. Minor transgressions are not punished by termination or forced resignation. Arguments, judgments, and decisions are rendered in the privacy of board meetings and generally remain confidential, as personnel matters are by law and tradition. Discussions are often heated. Facts are often in dispute, and interpretation of facts almost always disputed. While the final vote—often taken in public—may be unanimous, the real decision rarely is. Presidents almost always have at least a few supporters on the board who will support the majority to avoid publicity.

Among other things, boards consider the individual's past contributions to the institution and behavior on the job; the seriousness of the behavior that led to the possibility of termination or forced resignation; the likelihood that the offending behavior can be ameliorated and not repeated; and the potential for future significant leadership contribution.

Boards must always consider the effect a derailment will have on the morale of the campus community and the institution's public reputation. When a derailment becomes apparent or known, the institution will be perceived as having failed in an important way. Stories about why the president failed will abound—some true, some false, some both true and false. Many will be propagated by people who have a stake in the outcome, but some will be leaked by people who have an incomplete view of the reasons and causes. The public's perception of the institution is likely to nosedive, which may then entail an expensive public relations campaign. But, the alternative to a derailed president's departure—retaining a profoundly damaged or fatally flawed president—is equally problematic for the institution.

An important board function is to create the conditions that will enable the new president and his or her administration to succeed. Yet, some board behaviors undermine this responsibility. Weak or imperial chairs, who are likely to enable aberrant presidential behavior, are anathema to good governance. So is ignoring the broad principles of board responsibility for institutional governance. Boards can disempower presidents and disable institutions through micromanagement; by duplicitous or dishonest behavior; by seeking to meet with students, faculty, and staff independently rather than through appropriate committees and meetings; by advocating and funding personal hobbyhorses, rather than adhering to the institution's strategic goals that they are responsible for advancing and monitoring. Board members can chip away at the institution's integrity by seeking contracts for their companies, family, or friends, creating clear cases of conflict of interest masquerading as benevolent concern. They may even seek to influence the admission or graduation of students (qualified or not), believing that their position on the board entitles them to such consideration.

Boards are obliged, as a body and as individuals, to become familiar with good governance and the principles of academic freedom and free inquiry, as well as the particular culture of their institution, its history, mission, and aspirations. As higher education all too frequently has failed to develop programs to socialize new faculty, so too have boards ignored their responsibility to develop orientation programs to acquaint new board members with the culture of academia and the traditions of their individual institution or system. The board should also devote attention to reminding continuing board members of the obligations, limits, and constraints on their power and authority. In short, boards must also be forever vigilant in practicing good governance. Presidents must think about how best to engage the talents and relationships of board members to avoid temptations to create work that is unnecessary or counterproductive.

Unhappy Boards

Happy families are all alike; every unhappy family is unhappy in its own way.
                                                    LEO TOLSTOY, *Anna Karenina*

What Tolstoy wrote about families is true of boards as well. High-performing boards are more or less alike. Their policies and procedures comport with the guidelines proposed by the Association of Governing Boards of Universities and Colleges and other organizations dedicated to improving governance (see table 1.6). Roles are clearly delineated for board members and professionals charged with executing the strategy and tactics of the institution. Board work is conducted in an open, inclusive fashion. Committees diligently discharge their duties without usurping the full board's role in making decisions. While transparency is fostered, personnel decisions, in particular, remain in the shadows to the institution's varied stakeholders.

Less fortunate boards may be unhappy in a variety of ways that contribute to presidential derailments. Boards may be given to overlooking character flaws if institutional goals are met or exceeded. Better the devil we know than the devil we don't know. Boards may be riven by factionalism—presidential loyalists become antagonistic to those who are intent on exercising fiduciary oversight. Even setting aside flawed search processes, more than half of the sixteen case studies demonstrated clear evidence of board shortcomings. Board dysfunction may be rooted in group dynamics, individual board member behavior, lack of clarity around the board's role, and lack of unity around the institution's priorities.

Board unhappiness may be rooted in group dynamics. A subset of the board (often the executive committee) may make decisions without consulting the remainder of the board, invoking exigency where in fact there was no need for haste. A cabal of board members may meet privately to advance an agenda. Remember Carol at Caroline College, whose executive committee kept her poor performance reports to itself (see chapter 2). Board members may perpetuate a closed circle, reelecting the same officers year after year. Think of Daniel at Dogwood Community College (chapter 5), whose board had several members with more than twenty years of board service and caved easily to faculty calls for his dismissal.

Board unhappiness may be grounded in individual board member behavior. In advance of his formal interview at State University of the North, some board members—according to multiple reports—met privately with Nicholas, clearly violating search process protocol. Some chairs may act autocratically. Or, as happened to Michael at Medial College (chapter 2), the chair lets himself be manipulated by the past president. Some chairs—and presidents—retain control by not distributing materials sufficiently in advance of meetings for members to ponder them. Some board members never bother to read anything prior to the day of the meeting. Board members may be lackadaisical about attendance. Board members may pay more attention to their perquisites than their fiduciary duties.

Just as presidents can misplace their ethics, so can board members. Conflicts of interest, which seriously undermine board integrity, make it hard for presidents who try to do the right thing to succeed. At South Hogan University, Howard publicly battled board members who wanted the university to enter into a real estate agreement of uncertain value to the university with a wealthy donor (chapter 3). At Caroline College, investment committee members actively managed the endowment without having sought a request for proposals and the board chair was the college's legal counsel (chapter 2). These instances of questionable behavior, no doubt, created tension between the derailed president and board members.

Board unhappiness may arise also from lack of clarity and unity related both to institutional priorities and to board roles. Likewise, board members may not understand the lines of authority between their oversight and the president's management. Consider Antonio at Alpine Community College, whose board members were accustomed to awarding construction contracts and selecting academic deans (chapter 5). At Cypress Community College, after Calvin failed to renew a contract with a senior administrator's family's business, a board member met with upset employees without telling the president.

Some presidents have a different view of governance than the board and, in the spirit of shared governance in higher education, the faculty. At least half of the sixteen derailed presidents in the case studies did not have positive relationships with the faculty, many in the wake of institutional reorganizations. A few received a vote of no confidence. In fact, reports of no-confidence votes by faculty unions, faculty senates, or faculties as a whole have become more common as presidents and boards struggle with budget reductions mandated by the state or declining endowments. No-confidence votes often indicate unhappiness with the steps institutions took to ameliorate fiscal crises. In most cases, the board and president followed procedures laid out in institutional documents and consulted widely with campus constituents. Inevitably, some oxen were gored. Extensive consultation does not guarantee peaceful downsizing. Determining a college or university's most valuable programs is not easy, and boards have had to defend presidents and their own actions in the wake of difficult and unpopular decisions. Not every vote of no confidence should trigger a derailment. More often, they should prompt a wide and continuing discussion of the institution's mission, priorities, and process for decision making.

Differences of understanding, perspective, and priorities may also create subtle and not-so-subtle tensions between the president and the board. Alumni on the board may try to preserve the college as they remember it, be it from the 1950s or the 1990s. The president, of course, is focused on framing the future of the institution. Sally at University of the Southeast (chapter 4) moved fast and furiously through a difficult reorganization, leaving the board in her dust when they needed to be on the bus with her. The president may be juggling campus expectations from faculty and students against a mandate from the board. Especially during times of change, wise boards and presidents pay attention to the critical milestones for the institution and to key intersections in their relationship.

Unhappy boards take their toll on presidents. Sometimes, the board shortcomings are managed, massaged, or masked and the board-president relationship limps along. Other times, as demonstrated in the case studies, these board flaws exacerbate preexisting conditions and become one of several derailment symptoms. The challenge is to identify, cultivate, and maintain good governance practices that provide the right balance of support and supervision of the president.

Unhappy boards may find themselves in a perfect storm, as described in the section below called "What Can Go Wrong: A Case Study." The specific details of this case and the seemingly exaggerated circumstances of this college are beside the point. Far more important are the lessons for governance inherent in the case. Although the derailment did not occur during the president's first term of service, the derailment themes are identical to those in cases where the president has served for more than one term. The details of the case, which occurred at a well-known and prestigious institution, are instructive particularly because they show the interaction of several derailment themes.

What Can Go Wrong: A Case Study

A college selects a president after a protracted search. Just before the contract takes effect, the president-in-waiting informs the board that he cannot accept the job. The board then selects a less qualified candidate who wins the board's confidence by demonstrating intelligence and charm.

The new president is committed to transparent governance and operations and has a compelling vision for the future of the institution. He's off to a good start, working with the board to select trustees with time, talent, and treasure. The college improves year over year in terms of selectivity and fundraising.

The president's character starts to change. He persuades the board that his ex-officio status as a member of the board should include voting rights. Reluctantly, the board agrees. The president becomes a full member of the governance committee and begins extending invitations to board service without consulting the committee. As a voting member of the board, the president remains present during discussion of his compensation. The president begins to exhibit self-aggrandizing behaviors. He indulges in expenditures that further his personal stature, rather than that of the college. Events at the president's residence rarely include students, faculty, staff, or trustees, yet household expenses are charged to the college. Expenses are claimed for academic meetings and professional events that never occurred.

Despite an audit that revealed widespread financial indiscretion, the president's contract was renewed on existing terms and included an appropriate but modest salary increase, with full board support. Later, the board discovers that the chair had negotiated a new contract with the president that included a significant increase in his salary and expense account.

The college continues to grow in reputation and endowment. A majority of trustees are beholden to the president for their position on the board. His transgressions are overlooked, despite objections from a minority of trustees.

In the wake of this perfect storm, the president departed and several trustees resigned.

An Ounce of Prevention: Plan the Presidential Transition

The derailments described in this book all took place before the end of the president's first contract, a painful reminder that institutional turning points are delicate moments. While the board may feel like its work has been completed after the new president is named, the transition is only half finished.

The board has an ongoing responsibility for managing executive transitions in academic institutions. This responsibility requires as much attention to institutional culture as it does to oversight, and the board and president should pay attention to critical turning points (see table 8.1).

The following six suggestions for managing a presidential transition are based on insights from sitting board chairs and newly appointed presidents:

1. Manage campus anxieties with care
2. Understand that every presidency is different
3. See and seize a presidential transition as a refreshing moment of opportunity
4. Keep emphasizing the ongoing nature of the transition
5. Pave the way with planning
6. Invest in on-boarding resources and activities

MANAGE CAMPUS ANXIETIES WITH CARE

First, the executive transition begins the moment the president announces his departure, privately and then publicly. This means that everything the outgoing president and the board do will be examined under the microscope of institutional uncertainty. Depending on the nature of the current president's departure, an interim president or acting chief executive can help prepare the campus for a new president, reach out to constituents, and identify key institutional issues.

To pave the way for the new president and mitigate against a derailment, the board needs to manage both the departure of the outgoing president and the arrival of the incoming president. Pay attention to rituals, both for the outgoing and incoming presidents. Obviously, the pomp and circumstance of campus events and communications need to be attuned to the nature of the change. But, ceremonial farewells and subsequent welcoming festivities are important for emotional reasons and for a wide range of constituencies.

UNDERSTAND THAT EVERY PRESIDENCY IS DIFFERENT

Second, presidents and board members need to be aware that presidencies are like snowflakes. Each is unique. As we saw in six of the sixteen case studies, it is difficult to follow a long-standing or beloved president; just ask Ben at Beneficial College (chapter 2), Sally at University of the Southeast (chapter 4), Brandon at Birch Community College (chapter 5). There are aspects of ev-

Table 8.1.   Critical turning points in the board-president relationship

- Initial agreement to work together to bring about positive change
- Joint commitment to a plan of action
- Expression of unqualified support in the face of pushback from the faculty and external groups
- Steps to restore trust and respect in the relationship after a strain
- An endgame that anticipates the close of the liaison

Source: MacTaggart (2011)

ery presidency and institution that neither repeat presidents nor first-timers can anticipate. As one recently appointed president observed, "Stepping into a new institution feels like renting a car. You're not quite used to it."

Despite a long and arduous search process, the interviewing doesn't end for presidents once they are hired. Starting with his or her arrival on campus, a new president begins a second, more intense round of testing. Incoming presidents can and should position themselves as different from their predecessors, and they need the board's understanding and support in doing this.

Seize a Presidential Transition as a Refreshing Moment of Opportunity

Third, presidential transitions are good times for reflection and refreshment. They present the board with an opportunity to reconnect to other institutional stakeholders—faculty, students, alumni, donors, athletic boosters, and the local community. Conversations and connections should be driven through exploration of the institution's mission and vision for the future. The board, too, should use the transition to examine its own practices, behaviors, and composition. Every time a new person joins the "team," the whole team has to adjust. For example, a board retreat—perhaps held after the new president has spent a year on campus—might offer the board, president, and cabinet an opportunity to share notes from their different perspectives.

Keep Emphasizing the Ongoing Nature of the Transition

Fourth, especially in the beginning, it helps facilitate the process when institutional leaders remind each other and their constituents that the institution is in the midst of a transition. Publicly, the board should articulate the key milestones in the process, from search to appointment to on-boarding. More privately, with the new president, they should establish clear and realistic expectations and a reasonable timeframe, and they should review these goals periodically as the transition unfolds.

Pave the Way with Planning

Fifth, the board can support the new president through careful planning sessions—planning for orientation and on-boarding, planning for introductions to the different constituencies, planning for how to handle the annual budgeting and operating planning cycle. The board can help facilitate the transition if it has processes and policies in place that can be refined upon the arrival of the president. For presidents, especially, that first year is incredibly intense. They want to have a long-term vision, but they also need to know what they must do today and tomorrow—all while learning their way around a new campus, literally and figuratively. Table 8.2 offers a series of presidential self-reflection questions.

Beware, however, the itch to start strategic planning before a new president arrives (or on his or her first day). A new president can learn a lot just by observing and listening to stakeholders. Strategic planning is a powerful tool for a new leader to engage with the entire campus in shaping a shared dream for the institution. Ideally, under the direction of a new president, an inclusive strategic planning process that includes a review of the mission statement will pay tribute to the institution's past and carry it into the future.

Invest in On-boarding Resources and Activities

Finally, we have provided suggestions about what to do and what not to do during the so-called honeymoon period. But, the honeymoon may be short, in part because people at the institution will besiege the new president expecting him or her to grant their wishes. Boards can help by creating an appropriate discretionary budget that allows a new president to say "yes" in a variety of ways, early in the administration.

Providing on-boarding coaching is another form of support that can be helpful. For example, a first-time president might benefit from media training. Board members might also personally introduce a newcomer in town to the local leaders in the local community. They might provide copies of this book or others written that provide constructive advice and luminous examples about the challenges and rewards of higher education leadership. The board might set aside time and resources for a retreat sometime toward the end of the new president's first year.

Table 8.2.   Ten questions for leaders in transition

Discover (first 30–60 days)

1. What do you need to learn and how will you learn it?
2. How is the new role different from past roles, and what unique value can you bring to it?
3. What is the carryover from your predecessor and how will it impact you?
4. What lessons from past transitions—your own and others'—are relevant?

Define (second 30–60 days)

5. What are your "vital few" areas of focus for the first 12 months?
6. What performance indicators would you intend others use to assess you?

Deliver (remainder of first year)

7. Which of your leadership behaviors will help, or hinder, in the transition?
8. How will you develop the team needed to deliver on your transition plan?
9. What are the potential derailers for you and your group?

Build (all of first year)

10. Who are your stakeholders and how will you partner with them?

Source: Shaw and Chayes (2011).

Evaluating Effectiveness and Effective Evaluations

In the case studies, several of the derailed presidents either did not receive formal performance evaluations or the evaluations were not used as opportunities to address concerns and enhance executive performance. If it does not already have a formalized presidential evaluation process, the board should outline a review cycle that includes formal and informal feedback, especially during the critical first two years of a new president's tenure.

There is much to commend the periodic appraisal of the president. As a formal policy and practice, it is a tangible demonstration of the relationship between the board and the president. As a management practice, an annual performance review provides an established point in time to reflect on the past year and look to the next one.

The real value of performance appraisals, however, varies in practice. When they are done with limited input by stakeholders, not shared appropriately (or, on the other extreme, not closely held as a confidential personnel matter), they can be meaningless or even detrimental. Michael, the derailed president at Medial College, had received annual performance reviews and an A rating from the board. So, he was stunned when he received a call from the board chair asking for his resignation, especially since he had not had an evaluation that year (chapter 2).

A sound employment contract will reflect an agreement between the president and the board on institutional goals, measures of merit, and how success will be assessed and rewarded. More specifically, the president's contract should provide for an annual performance assessment by an appropriate board committee. Appraisal systems are manifestations of institutional philosophy and priorities, of what will be valued in leader performance. A formal performance appraisal helps make the criteria, expectations, and evidence of effectiveness operational.

Presidential evaluations in academic institutions often begin with agreed upon performance goals. Drawing on the corporate model of management by objectives, the president is evaluated on performance goals that were accomplished during a specified period of time (usually a year). These goals are usually developed by the president in collaboration with the board (or a committee of the board). The evaluation process should include institutional and individual goals. At the end of the year, the president and board may share a presidential report card with the campus community. This report card summarizes metrics and marks of accomplishment against the established set of executive goals and objectives. Early in a president's tenure, progress toward accomplishment of mutually agreed upon goals is more likely than goal achievement.

Part of a president's formal evaluation review should include feedback from representatives of these constituencies about the president's relationship with them, not just their assessment of his performance. The purpose of this input is to inform the board of the president's ability to lead the whole institution. A 360-degree evaluation offers a deeper sense of a president's performance. It involves input from stakeholders above (e.g., the board), below (e.g., cabinet members), and to the side (e.g., deans, faculty, etc.) of the president. A wide variety of 360-degree evaluation tools are available, from customizable online surveys to institutionally developed templates.

As the president becomes more fully integrated into the institution, the board and president may decide that an externally facilitated evaluation provides a more meaningful assessment. An objective, external consultant (sometimes a peer from another institution) will gather feedback—often using a combination of surveys and interviews—from representatives of stakeholder groups, such as faculty, board, civic leaders, external community members (such as affiliated clergy), government or political liaisons, or corporate officers. The findings are summarized into a comprehensive report that the board uses in providing feedback to the president. Some boards ask for an external evaluation during the second year of incumbency, but this may be premature, unless the board has reason to believe that the marriage is headed for the rocks.

Presidential performance evaluations are the paramount personnel matter for the board, and they need to be handled with the right balance between respect for confidentiality and disclosure for appropriate board oversight. The full board has a role to play in the president's performance evaluation, both providing input and approving the conclusions. A committee (executive, compensation, personnel) or an individual (such as the chair) may facilitate the process, but—except in the most urgent or dire circumstances—the committee should not need to act on behalf of the full board. The designated committee or individual should make recommendations rather than final determinations. The entire board has responsibility for hiring, compensating, and if necessary firing the president. In order to carry out those responsibilities in a prudent manner, all board members must have access to relevant information. For the greater good of the institution, presidents should not fear transparency and boards should insist on it.

The Dashboard: A Tool Tracking Progress and Performance

As one component in assessing presidential performance, many boards use a dashboard that indicates the status and trend line of key institutional metrics. Dashboards show where progress is being made and where the institution is faltering. As an Educause Center for Applied Research bulletin explains:

> Factors such as student recruitment and admission, teaching load, graduation rates, staff turnover, generated funds, and proposal-to-award ratios affect a university's performance. However, few higher education institutions are able to capture and report their many data points on all levels. A digital dashboard is a management tool for setting and measuring expectations at every organizational level, with easy-to-understand charts and reports of the status of progress throughout the year. (Harel and Sitko, 2003)

Dashboards come highly recommended, but they must be used with sensitivity. They should provoke analysis, not become a bludgeon. Rising scores on the dashboard may reflect deliberate action, externally caused change, or a blip. Likewise, declining scores may reflect a lack of action, an externally caused change, or a transient departure from the norm. Reacting to monthly or quarterly changes is generally ill advised. Trends, not snapshots, are important and must be considered within the context in which the institution operates. That context includes not only the local, regional, and national economic health but also that of peer institutions.

For example, regression in and of itself is not necessarily a sign of poor presidential performance. Mitigating factors must be considered. For example, alumni contributions may fall short of projections, but a global recession makes that understandable, albeit lamentable. Student retention may be declining but, without knowing the root causes, blaming the president is less valuable than asking what strategies he or she has proposed to overcome the problem. Applications may be down, but that may be a national trend. More important, the board needs to consider whether that is a meaningful or trivial measure of presidential—not to mention institutional—success. As the chief executive officer, the president has responsibility for the entire institution, but the board needs to be thoughtful and judicious about evaluating the president.

Boards will find dashboards helpful though not dispositive. They may provide early warning, but they are more likely to be useful in framing the annual assessment and the discussion between the appropriate members of the board and the president about institutional and individual performance. Presidents who use dashboards find them helpful in taking action to halt adverse trends. Boards might most fruitfully ask whether the president is using the dashboard in a timely fashion to guide action.

Informal Feedback

Too many derailments are also the result of unfortunate behavior patterns by presidents—bad tempers, profligate spending, inappropriate relationships. Dashboards will not reveal those transgressions. Boards need to make certain that they have a way of evaluating institutional climate. This is no easy task under normal circumstances, but it is further complicated because board members may not appreciate the complexities of a president's professional and personal lives—the incessant nature of demands and demanders, the fact that there is more good to be done than there are resources to do them, the volatile landscape of higher education, the enormous costs of keeping up with changes in technology and applying them to the fundamental institutional purposes of instruction, service, and research.

Frequent and regular contact between the president, board chair, and executive committee is another useful way to provide ongoing feedback. Informal meetings, open exchanges, and confidential conversations should supplement more formal reporting occasions, like quarterly board meetings. Board committees should work with appropriate members of the administration and campus community to gain a sense of the texture of institutional life. Complaining voices are more likely to be heard than satisfied ones. Persistent and general complaints may indicate the need for attention or action; occasional complaints or missteps may not. A dashboard can be useful in determining which is which. By creating a continuous feedback loop, the board and president can address issues as they arise and make midcourse corrections.

The Special Role of the Board Chair

The leadership style and qualities of the board chair determine how well the group works together and whether ground rules about appropriate behavior and interaction with administrators, faculty, staff, and students are followed or flouted. Successful chairs keep members focused on policy and strategy rather than insisting on consultation on every decision a president is called on to make; ensure that board committees and members undertake their written charges and other tasks promptly and thoroughly; abjure gossip and innuendo; get and give factual information from and to board members; work with the administration to provide board members agendas and other materials well in advance of meetings and insist that members prepare for meetings by reading those materials; and collaborate with the president to inspire the campus and the community as they are the two primary public faces of the institution (excluding the football and basketball coaches, of course).

Successful board chairs involve themselves in the life of the institution; they ensure that the board includes members who can provide continuity as well as those who bring fresh vision and insight to their work. Successful chairs communicate with the president frequently and informally, and they develop with the president appropriate ways of evaluating the performance of the institution and its leadership. They spearhead fundraising. They embrace transparency and accountability.

Unsuccessful board chairs are not collaborative except perhaps with a small group of members; do not share important information with the board; usurp the role of the president by indulging in micromanagement; fail to develop relevant measures of merit for board member performance and the performance of the president; and receive and spread gossip and rumor. Unsuccessful board chairs do not balance well the roles of institutional cheerleader and institutional overseer. They meddle in or condone cronyism in board membership, in institutional contracting, and in hiring faculty and staff. Their institutional giving is niggling. Members of boards will take their cues from the board chair, who models their behaviors toward the president, their colleagues, the community, and the faculty, students, and staff.

A president who has been successful at five institutions wrote us that presidential success is unlikely without a working collegial partnership with board chairs who demonstrate in their daily work passion, courage, imagination, vision, institutional loyalty, executive leadership, mentorship, and unimpeachable integrity. A board chair combats fate, time, occasion, chance, and change with patience, virtue, wisdom, and endurance.

Fortunately for American higher education, most board chairs are successful and exhibit the qualities we have enumerated. That doesn't mean there won't be presidential derailments during their watch. Some derailments are in the best interest of the institution. But many, too many, are the result of friction between the board (especially the chair) and the president. Too many could have been prevented by adopting and adapting the practices we present in this book.

Conclusion: The Intricate Board-President Dance

The case studies also reveal that the derailed presidents had difficulty leading key constituencies. Whether it was communicating with board members, leading the cabinet, or working with the faculty, many of the derailed presidents failed to develop strategic relationships with key stakeholders. While guiding the institution down a new strategic path, implementing a difficult reorganization, or responding to negative publicity, they were stranded and left alone on the side of the road because they had no social capital on which to draw and no buffer to shield them from their critics.

The relationship between the board and the president is an intricate dance; a bolero or pasodoble—at times the partners are close together, at other times distance lends enchantment to the view. Like all relationships, those between the board and a president are dynamic. Vector and momentum must be aligned but will not always be in harmony. Prolonged dissonance is cause for alarm, as is its absence.

Chapter Nine

Lessons Learned about Presidential Derailments

Human Imperfection

Humans are complex constellations of intellect, personality, and character. The promise of nobility and duplicity is carried in the heart and mind of each individual. This valence in human behavior was recognized by the architects of the U.S. Constitution, who placed in that document a provision for impeachment before the first president was elected—a form of presidential derailment policy. Optimism about the human spirit was married to the possibility of wayward behavior, and a proper response to such behavior anticipated.

The visibility and scope of responsibility of academic presidents magnify honorable behavior and wrongdoing, great leadership and weak management. College, university, and system presidents hold in trust the institutions expected to prepare leaders for every sector of our national life. The humanity of presidents and the humanity of board members suggest that not every derailment, and its attendant financial and reputational cost, is preventable. But, higher education can, should, and must do better.

The six derailment themes demarcated in this book are pervasive in the academy, as well as in business, industry, and government. Two themes fall squarely on the shoulder of presidents themselves—(1) ethical lapses and (2) poor interpersonal skills—and may be insurmountable. Three themes reside in the context and culture of each institution—(3) inability to lead key constituents, be they the board, cabinet, faculty, or government officers; (4) difficulty adapting to a new industry, institution, position, or community; and (5) failure to meet business objectives, such as budget numbers, fundraising goals, or student enrollment. The final theme, (6) board shortcomings, includes several distinct variations, from flawed searches and conflicts of interest to micromanaging and dysfunctional group dynamics.

While these six derailment themes may not constitute the whole truth for all presidential derailments, they emerged from well-established management theory and in-depth research of the academic institutions profiled in this book and others we have studied. They also accord with our own experience in presidents' offices of public and private sector institutions of higher education and with the widespread media coverage of presidential failures. They merit the attention of board members, presidents, senior administrators, government representatives, and anyone interested in the presidency.

What lessons can we derive from the research and the experiences presented in this book? While there are certain realities that boards and presidents cannot change, they can put in place good or better leadership, governance, and management practices to minimize the possibility of an early derailment.

The Board's Realities

The most fundamental reality is that presidential selection, as in all hiring decisions, remains a process subject to complex personal and environmental factors that cannot be entirely predicted or controlled. A 100 percent positive record on presidential appointment and performance is not probable. Thus, the goal is not selection perfection but risk mitigation—identifying and minimizing the more obvious errors that warrant more careful board attention.

Second, boards are leadership teams that, in athletic parlance, play but rarely practice—convening infrequently for the game time of board meetings. Boards are comprised of well-meaning and busy individuals with unique and important external perspectives but with bounded knowledge of the institution. Against this backdrop, difficult decisions—hiring or firing the president—are even more complicated. In such moments, not just good, but great board leadership and processes are particularly important.

Third, many factors related to presidential derailment may be traced not only to the unfortunate behavior of the president and board but also to unwarranted political meddling by still other voices. An academic institution's external environment may include governors, legislators, business executives, or religious leaders attempting to influence a presidential search or institutional priorities for personal or ideological interests. Boards that inadvertently permit or deliberately insert political interests into a search process should not be surprised at the negative fallout from such careless or duplicitous behavior.

Fourth, the democratic principle that all authority is invested in the consent of the governed also applies to institutions of higher education. College and universities are distinguished from corporate enterprise by the complexity of their missions, governance structures, and intended outcomes. They have many legitimate and important stakeholders. To ignore their voices, at least in some representative sense, during the search process promotes the probability of derailment down the road.

Finally, the same political reality applies after a new president is installed and the next phase of work begins: leading, managing, and governing an academic institution. Different campus constituents—faculty, governors, major donors, board cabals, community leaders—may attempt to pursue narrowly framed, self-serving agendas. The board, if it can rise above the fray, is in the best position to make sure that the institution's long-term interests take precedence.

The Position of President

Presidencies come with a multitude of constituents, each with legitimate claim to voice on institutional purpose, policy, and performance. Board members, however, retain the premier voice among these diverse stakeholders. From the first day in office, a president discovers the many cooks in the kitchen. Every decision runs the risk of creating one ingrate and dozens of people who are resentful. Presidents must dine with those wearing sandals and tennis shoes and with those wearing wing tips and silken pumps. They must inspire but not make promises they cannot keep. They must cultivate and retain their colleagues' trust while seeking a wide variety of advice and opinion but also be willing to keep with the "perfect sweetness the independence of solitude" amidst the crowd, as Emerson noted. They must be willing to be lonely for what they believe to be right in the face of a countervailing majority.

Presidencies come with boundaries, whether they are the top of the organizational chart as chief executive delegating responsibilities or at the bottom as servant leader holding in trust the promise of an academic institution. They must occasionally say "no" to very good ideas because of limited resources or bad timing. There are more good programs and services than can be accomplished even at the richest institutions. Presidents should be the institutional leader with the widest, most informed perspective. While, as Harry Truman observed, many bucks stop in the presidential suite, many ideas and initiatives are also affirmed there.

Presidencies require patience, persistence, and energy. Presidents rarely punch an eight-hour time clock. They expect to invest long hours in the challenges before them and the institution or system. Presidencies take time to flourish. An article in the *Wall Street Journal* (July 6, 2010, B5) pointed out that twenty-five of the twenty-eight CEOs who have held the title for more than fifteen years "have seen their company's total shareholder return . . . exceed the S&P 500 index performance during their tenures." Five of the seven CEOs whose companies underperformed the market during their first three years eventually exceeded it.

The same may be true for presidents of academic institutions. If higher education leaders want good things to happen, they need to be in the harness for the long run, as academic institutions are large ships with a momentum of their own. They can, however, gradually shift direction, with patient tending and use of a small rudder. If presidents and boards want constructive change—change that will endure beyond the individuals—then they must labor for the long term. Otherwise, once the presidential thumb is taken off the button, progress will evaporate.

Last, we need to recognize that a president may be derailed for acting both competently and ethically in the legitimate service of institutional goals and welfare but in doing so may confront the dissenting interest of powerful stakeholders, such as board members, government officials, religious leaders, or corporate constituents. Experience and research indicate that board members acting in service of duplicitous or self-interested goals put their institutions in harm's way.

Politics and the Presidency

Colleges and universities are not immune to political forces and influence, nor should they be. Politics, in this context, means the use of influence and the art of being personal. A critical leadership challenge for presidents is managing contending influences. A board or external constituency that attempts to make the institution an instrument of political will sets the stage for instability, for retribution, and for the smothering of truth and trust as the winds of political and ideological influence shift. Academic institutions must remain anchored to broader social and civic interests. Interpreting and balancing those interests is a stewardship function of the board, with support from the president. Colleges and universities can become political hockey pucks, slapped back and forth between conflicting interests that have forgotten what a precious instrument of democracy, what a guarantor of openness and transparency, they hold in trust.

Especially in public institutions, board shortcoming may stem from politics. At one extreme, a governor who disagrees with the president may replace all or enough board members to derail the president (as happened to Brandon at Birch Community College in chapter 5). Less obvious, boards of public universities and systems may be insufficiently independent from the governor or legislators. They may be driven by a different agenda (e.g., state budgets, job creation, political parties) and make decisions that are detrimental to the institution whose health they are charged to maintain and improve. In some cases, state legislatures may usurp the powers generally vested in regents for example, by approving a new academic program without board involvement.

At public institutions that are part of a statewide system, presidents and boards must find a path that allows for continuous improvement of their institution while remaining cognizant of the authority of a board responsible for the health of the system as a whole. That is sufficiently challenging in good economic times. In tough times, competition for dwindling resources may lead faculties, staff, students, and alumni to blame the president and the board for any diminution in budget or program. Likewise, board and executive leaders of state systems are likewise held responsible for the failure of legislatures to fund higher education at the level to which the faculty, staff, and students have become accustomed.

Personalities and the Presidency

Not all presidential derailments are matters of great mystery. A president who engages in an extramarital affair with a staff member, one who misuses public funds, one whose leadership style borders on abusive, these are instances where a board will want to be thoughtful but not reticent in "pulling the plug," where surgery may be more effective than hope, patience, or forgiveness.

However, some mysteries linger, as evidenced by the research and experi-

The Chancellor and the Governor
E. Grady Bogue

In 1982, during my second year as chancellor of Louisiana State University Shreveport, oil prices plummeted and the state budget took a serious hit. When Republican Governor Dave Treen announced projected budget cuts for all agencies, including higher education, the Baton Rouge *Advocate* called chancellors and presidents to get their reactions. The next morning, I was quoted as saying that we appreciated the fiscal pressures faced by the state and governor and that we would do our best to support his efforts to manage the budget crisis.

After the story appeared, Shelley Beychock, chair of the LSU Board of Supervisors and former chair of the Louisiana Democratic Party, called me to say he was convening a special board meeting to request that the governor exempt higher education from the proposed cuts. He further suggested that repeating what I said to the reporter would do little to engender the board action he wanted. "If called upon by the board to comment on the proposed cuts," I replied to Shelley, "I will lay the facts on the table and report what steps we would take to accommodate the cuts."

At the board meeting, each chancellor was asked to comment on the effect of the proposed cuts. Comments were filled with a mix of emotion, exaggeration, and fact. When my turn came, I explained that we would freeze travel, equipment and library purchases, and vacant positions. At the end of the meeting, the LSU board voted against chair Beychock's proposal to exempt LSU from the cuts.

A few months later, I read a story in the *Shreveport Times* that Republican Governor Treen planned to relieve Northwestern State University in Natchitoches of a portion of its cuts. Furious, I immediately composed a press release expressing my disappointment that no other university was given similar treatment. I also noted that I was able to come to one of two conclusions: Either Northwestern was suffering from severe management and fiscal problems or that the LSU board had made a mistake in not asking to be relieved of the cuts.

I then arranged lunch with Dalton Woods, a successful oil company owner, member of the LSU board, and an influential Republican. When I shared the proposed press release, Woods indicated that candor was the order of the day and advised me to issue the statement. The next day, the *Shreveport Times* front page carried this headline: "Bogue Questions Governor."

I stood in the middle of the political aisle, having been given advice by the Democratic board chair and soon to receive advice from the Republican vice chair. At the next LSU board meeting, I was beckoned to a tête-à-tête with vice chair John Cade, another very influential Republican. I asked Woods to accompany me across the room to chat with Cade. Cade suggested that some folks felt I had hung the governor out in the wind. Before I could respond, Woods jumped in and suggested that Cade may have forgotten my first statement supporting the governor's fiscal challenge, the LSU board's vote not to request an exemption from these cuts, and Cade's vote for that motion.

Throughout all this, LSU Shreveport had a $12-million capital proposal awaiting the governor's signature. A few weeks later, at a civic dinner, I was invited to a brief private conversation with the governor. Governor Treen was friendly, indicating that he was sorry he had not been able to call me personally but that I could appreciate all the alligators in the swamp. He confidentially confirmed my assumption about serious problems at Northwestern. I responded, "I appreciate your taking the time to visit with me, and we will continue to do our best to support you. Governor, will you sign my capital outlay building project?" He replied, "Don't worry about it, you'll get your building."

This is a story of more than politics. It is a story of relationships, relationships that began when I first arrived in Louisiana and met individually with each board member. It is a story of candor, speaking truth to power, and trying to do the right thing. Finally, it is a story of leverage, of leveraging individual board member relationships with me and with one another for the greater good. This story has a happy ending. Not all do. The ending, however, is not the issue. Leadership choice is. Every choice we make writes our own leadership story. Nobility of character depends not on being dealt a favorable hand, but on playing whatever hand is dealt with honor and integrity.

Adapted from Bogue 2007.

---

ences of derailed presidencies. How can a presidential candidate show sufficient brilliance in intellect and in previous performance to be considered a likely candidate for a presidency and then become such a cultural and interpersonal disaster following the appointment? The following questions are designed to offer constructive guidance to new presidents in the hopes of avoiding mistakes that may lead to derailment.

Why would a new president request letters of resignation from all senior staff so that she may decide who stays and who goes?
This act represents such a monumental reflection of insecurity that it is hardly credible to see some new presidents still make this form of entrance. Such an act makes no use of the power of great expectations, well established in

the literature as an important leadership principle. Instead, it casts a pall of suspicion and mistrust over the institution. Such an act assumes pathology rather than health in an institution and its people.

Why would a new president not start by sitting down personally with major stakeholder groups—the board, key faculty, student and staff groups, with community leaders?

As Yogi Berra noted, "you can observe a lot by watching." Likewise, you can learn a lot by listening. Informal settings are perfect starting points for a new president to understand the institution from different perspectives, to begin building relationships, to identify action and policy priorities, to demonstrate the values of openness and engagement. How else can or should a new president begin to discern, identify, and shape personal expectations and institutional priorities? A new president should not be devoid of some vision of what he or she sees as both promises and challenges for the institution. Indeed, we would worry about a leader whose head and heart were empty of ideas and conviction. For a vision to take hold at an institution, however, it needs to be carefully orchestrated and to draw on a broad base of allegiance and support. Such a collective journey begins with the president listening to those whose energy, talent, and devotion will translate a shared dream into a shared reality.

Why would a new president not walk slowly around campus, listening to those within and without, learning about the dreams and pains of those who have been there before him?

Failure in interpersonal relationships and failure to build a team get frequent attention in these stories of derailment. A new president, in fact all presidents, need to nurture social capital with those who are entrusted to his leadership and with whom he will work in the months and hopefully years to come. A new president needs to show up in the boiler rooms and the power towers and to appear in unexpected places and times to affirm the role and contribution of each and every person in the campus community. Metaphors of role are not small matters because these metaphors become shorthand theories by which presidential behavior is guided. Presidents do not own their institutions, and so the metaphors of stewardship and servant-leader are commanding anchors.

Why would a new president, with a highly successful career and in a highly public position, fall prey to the temptations of power?

In his brilliant little book, *Leadership Is an Art*, Max De Pree (De Pree,

1989, p. 9) offers a succinct and compelling guide to effective leadership. Truly understanding and internalizing these two lines is more than worth the cost of the book:

1. "The first responsibility of the leader is to define reality. The second is to say 'Thank you.'"
2. "Style is merely a consequence of what we believe."

Compassion, courage, candor, civility—the guide of good values—is not complex. Morality is written in bold letters by those who are expected to be exemplars (another good metaphor) before their boards, faculty and staff members, students, donors, athletic boosters, and community leaders.

Why would a new president waver in "speaking truth to power" on issues related to academic excellence and institutional integrity?

The new president might as well learn whether those to whom he or she reports are open to thoughtful and honest dissent or whether they consider those who disagree as folks without proper parents. Then, the president can decide whether to shape and influence the climate and values of the institution or whether to vacate the position.

Why would a new president not take the time to learn the culture of an institution before taking up broom, shovel, and wrench to make wholesale changes?

The derailment narratives in this work point to new presidents not understanding or unnecessarily violating culture. New presidents would do well to heed the dictum: Learn first, and do later. Along with leaders in other enterprises, presidents and chancellors have three responsibilities for culture: to affirm culture, to challenge culture, and to create culture. All of these, however, begin with taking the time to understand an institution's heritage and habits. If the existing culture is detrimental or destructive to human promise and performance, then the new president can and should challenge that culture and lead the institution in creating a better one. In many cases, new presidents will contribute to the creation of constructive cultural attributes.

Lessons Learned

The reasons for presidential derailments are relatively few in number and persistent. Presidents today lose their positions for the same reasons that presidents lost their positions in the past. And, they lose them for the same reasons as do politicians, corporate executives, and religious leaders.

Why haven't today's presidents learned from those who came before? Perhaps they have studied the lessons and still ignore them—a disconnect between conviction and courage. It cannot be that they don't know what behaviors lead to derailment. But, they act as though the lessons apply only to those not as clever or talented as they are. "I'm too smart to get caught" supplants ethical judgments and abnegates the super ego.

Freud famously defined "exceptions" as those people who believe, often unconsciously, that they are entitled to pursue the pleasure principle and ignore the reality principle. Examples are both manifold and egregious. Consider the general who was in charge of a leadership course that all newly selected general officers and senior executives were obliged to take. One of the lessons repeated throughout the course was that sexual misbehavior would surely get you fired if you were found out. The general teaching the course was demoted and retired after commanders determined that he sexually harassed female subordinates, engaged in unprofessional behavior, and created a hostile work environment.

We are under no illusion that the cases we have presented, the arguments we have advanced, the factors we have illuminated, and the solutions we recommend will put an end to presidential derailments. The "exceptions" will continue to behave in disruptive and self-destructive ways. But, the majority of derailments might be better managed. Many factors were within the president's control. One can choose and learn to be more humble and less imperial, more open and less aggressive, more welcoming of divergent opinions and less certain of one's own judgment, more ambitious for the future of the institution and less ambitious about one's own status.

Boards might benefit from better practices of board self-reflection, more thorough searches, and more thoughtful transition plans. The obvious starting point for boards is to design and implement a search process marked by openness and transparency, by integrity of process, by thorough investigation of candidate credentials, by inclusive representation of campus stakeholders. The end point should be a search dedicated to the future and the promise of the whole institution rather than to the personal or political interests of a small number of powerful people. There is no place for parlor soldiers on boards. Every board member must take responsibility for the success of the search process.

Can a board discover more about an individual's psychic makeup prior to selection? Can a board intervene successfully during the early months of a president's tenure to ensure that the presidential train stays on track? We've made suggestions. Some will help, but none are infallible. Boards cannot fruitfully ask a candidate "When did you stop beating your staff?" Executive coaching may prove helpful, but most often leopards cannot change their spots. Contracts with clear measures of merit and well-designed performance evaluation methods may help the board provide better support and supervision to a new president and perhaps ease a necessary departure, but they are unlikely to change fundamental patterns of individual behavior. Character and personality fissures may not reveal themselves until placed under the pressure of the presidency.

In Conclusion

The suggestions we offer are culled from the authors' own experience, from the research conducted by our collaborators, from the wise advice of practitioners, and from the literature on derailment. They are not a prescriptive all-or-nothing proposition, nor are they a guaranteed path to success. They are offered as ideas to be considered when initiating a search, after hiring a new president, and when hitting a proverbial bump in the road. Our goal with this book is to improve the probability of appointing and keeping presidents of academic institutions who serve with competence and integrity.

Here is the sum of the matter. Boards should celebrate the important responsibility invested to their care in selecting the president. They should heed the standards of good governance in their own practices and policies. Collectively and individually, each board member is accountable for both process and outcome. Presidents, for their part, should study carefully the play in which they have been cast to ensure that their values, experience, and knowledge are well suited for the role. They should expect their integrity, courage, and endurance to be tested, and they should be prepared to stand firm.

Boards and presidents may take pleasure that they hold in trust institutions that are central to human development, a cornerstone of the national economy, a curator of heritage, a seeker of truth, an enemy of injustice, and a guarantor of an open, transparent, and vibrant democracy.

Appendix

A Year of Presidential Turnover

> I have but one lamp by which my feet are guided, and that is the lamp of experience. I know no way of judging the future but by the past.
>
> EDWARD GIBBON

A derailed presidency can undermine a university's image, destroy school morale, and cost millions of dollars. Our research attempts to understand what goes wrong, and who in university leadership has the ability to address issues before situations irreparably deteriorate. When we are able to uncover the details of a derailment, the lessons we learn may guide the feet of future university leaders. However, more often than not, we have found the details are impossibly obscured.

When university presidents leave in turmoil, the negotiated settlement almost universally includes a confidentiality agreement. Beyond confidentiality agreements, troubled boards and school administrations usually erect a wall of silence, preventing outsiders from determining what actually happened. Neither the trustees nor the resigning president want the details of their failure or the cost of settlement paraded through the press. The university needs to move on from the crisis; the ex-president needs to continue his or her career. In the immediate aftermath, full public disclosure is in no one's best interest.

Years after the fact, the lessons we could learn from presidential derailments often remain hidden. Media reports provide incomplete and sometimes misleading information about precisely what happened. We are grateful that the individuals included in this book were willing to be forthright about their experiences; many of the parties we would have liked to include were either unwilling to risk talking to us or were bound to silence by confidentiality agreements.

The following appendix reveals certain patterns: Derailments happen throughout the academy. Seasoned leaders and new administrators alike stumble. No type or size of school is immune. And the information available from public media sources is often insufficient for understanding precisely what went wrong. Imagine the lessons we would learn if more information were available.

In 2009, twenty-five university presidents resigned, retired prematurely, or were fired. Of these, five retain their positions after faculty votes of no confidence. A few cases outlined below may not be derailments but were included because there is not enough information available publicly to make a clear determination.

Note: The individual institutions described below are classified according to the Carnegie classification system (Carnegie "Basic" classification). See classifications.carnegie foundation.org for more information.

Bruce Leslie
Chancellor, 2006 to present
Alamo Colleges (San Antonio, Texas)
Public Community College System
5 Schools
60,366 Students
When the board of trustees hired Leslie, it asked him to curtail wasteful spending and improve communications among the individual schools. Faculty members were upset when reforms resulted in increased class sizes, reduction in full-time faculty, and increased standardization. In September 2009, more than 90 percent of voting faculty favored a declaration of no confidence in Leslie.

Leslie resigned from the Connecticut Community College System in 1999 and from the Houston Community College System in 2006 after conflicts with school leaders and trustees. He remains chancellor of Alamo Colleges.

Jehuda Reinharz
President, 1994 to 2010
Brandeis University (Waltham, Massachusetts)
Carnegie Classification: Private not-for-profit; 4-year or above; Research Universities (very high research activity)
5,327 Students
After the 2008 financial crisis, donations to Brandeis dropped dramatically and the value of its investments decreased significantly. Faculty criticized Reinharz's financial stewardship. In January, the trustees' unanimous vote to auction the art collection and close the art museum angered faculty, students, and alumni groups.

Reinharz announced in September 2009 that he would resign at the end of the academic year and, at the request of trustees, remained in the job until a replacement assumed office on January 1, 2011.

Charles Reed
Chancellor, 1998 to present
California State University
Public University System
23 Schools
433,000 Students
California's state budget crisis led to deep cuts to its public universities. In July 2009, the California Faculty Association, the union representing the largest proportion of California State University faculty, voted to approve a two day per month unpaid furlough. At the same

time, union members overwhelmingly voted no confidence in the chancellor. Reed remains the Chancellor of the California State University System.

Hamid Shirvani
President, 2005 to present
California State University–Stanislaus (Turlock, California)
Carnegie Classification: Public; 4-year or above; Master's Colleges and Universities (larger programs)
8,601 Students
The California State University system faced severe budget deficits in 2009, and Cal State–Stanislaus received a $13.5-million cut to its budget. When 91 percent of eligible faculty voted for a no-confidence declaration in November of that year, faculty leaders cited financial troubles, public missteps, high administrator turnover, shared governance concerns, and an article Shirvani wrote criticizing the faculty culture throughout higher education.

Shirvani is still the president of California State University–Stanislaus.

Susan Kelly
President, 2006 to 2009
Charles Drew University of Medicine and Science (Los Angeles, California)
Carnegie Classification: Private not-for-profit; 4-year or above; Special Focus Institutions—Health professions schools
255 Students
When Kelly became president of Charles Drew University, it was in the midst of a scandal surrounding poor patient care in the hospital it ran in association with Los Angeles County. In 2007, the hospital severed its relationship with Charles Drew, and the university temporarily stopped accepting new students to its medical residency program. Kelly led a drive to expand programs and recover, but her reforms were hindered by the economic crisis.

In May 2009, Kelly announced suddenly that she would resign immediately. Both Kelly and trustees claimed that the resignation was voluntary.

David Pelham
President, 2008 to 2009
Cuesta College (San Luis Obispo, California)
Carnegie Classification: Public, 2-year; Associate's—Public Rural-serving, Large
11,341 Students
Weeks after signing a new three-year contract, Pelham abruptly announced that he would be leaving to become the director of Abu Dhabi Women's College.

During his tenure, Cuesta faced significant state budget cuts and a $6-million budget shortfall. In his resignation letter, Pelham indicated that he did not believe he could effectively lead Cuesta College. He balanced critiques of his own leadership with criticisms of an intransigent organizational culture at the college.

Robert Myers
President, 2005 to 2009
Daniel Webster College (Nashua, New Hampshire)
Carnegie Classification: Private, for-profit; 4-year or above; Baccalaureate Colleges—
Diverse Fields
1,007 Students
Daniel Webster College's endowment was relatively small, and the institution had limited resources to weather the economic downturn. By mid-2009, it was $23 million in debt.

In June of that year, ITT Educational Services, Inc., bought Daniel Webster College. In August, Myers was fired, along with another senior administrator, twenty-three staff members, and sixty other employees.

Jill Landesberg-Boyle
President, 2007 to 2009
Florida Keys Community College (Key West, Florida)
Carnegie Classification: Public; 2-year; Associate's—Public Rural-serving Small
1,208 Students
From the beginning, Landesberg-Boyle's administration was troubled. Anonymous sources repeatedly sent e-mails to the community attacking her leadership style and management skills. In her first two years, she replaced more than half of the full-time faculty. Detractors claimed Landesberg-Boyle created a toxic work environment; supporters argued that she was targeted by a corrupt political system. In public meetings, speakers were roughly evenly divided for and against the president. In 2008, the college tried private mediation, but it did not calm tensions.

In September 2009, Landesberg-Boyle agreed to take paid leave with benefits until the end of her contract term.

Horace Judson
President, 2004 to 2009
Grambling State University (Grambling, Louisiana)
Carnegie Classification: Public; 4-year or above; Master's Colleges and Universities (medium programs)
5,253 Students
After a series of contentious meetings with faculty and student leaders, Judson abruptly resigned, citing family reasons. Both the faculty senate and student government had considered no-confidence votes. Press reports list a variety of concerns, including mishandled student financial aid, an opaque budget process, and a $160,000 security fence around the president's residence.

Before becoming president of Grambling State University, Judson was president of Plattsburgh State University, where he resigned in 2003 after a faculty no-confidence vote.

Craven Williams
President, 1993 to 2009
Greensboro College (Greensboro, North Carolina)
Carnegie Classification: Private not-for-profit; 4-year or above; Baccalaureate Colleges—
Diverse Fields
1,279 Students
Greensboro College was hard-hit by the economic downturn; in April 2009, Williams cut salaries by 20 percent and was relying on loans to meet summer operating expenses. The faculty had considered a no-confidence vote, and the university required an extension to complete its 2007-8 audit.

On July 8, 2009, Williams announced he would retire, effective immediately.

Mark Drummond
Chancellor, 1999 to 2004, 2007 to 2009
Los Angeles Community College (Los Angeles, California)
Community College Network
9 Schools
141,215 Students
Drummond was unexpectedly placed on a leave of absence in June 2009, and resigned a few weeks later. He was to be paid $428,750 for the remaining twenty-three months of his contract and will keep his lifetime health insurance and retirement benefits. No reason was given for his exit, and his termination agreement included a strict confidentiality clause. Two of the school's campuses have since been placed on probation by accreditors.

Darnell Cole
President, 2001 to 2009
Milwaukee Area Technical College (Milwaukee, Wisconsin)
Carnegie Classification: Public; 2-year; Associate's—Public Urban-serving Multicampus
18,780 Students
In February 2009, Cole failed a field sobriety test and was ticketed for drunk driving. Two weeks later, the school's board of directors voted to fire him, effective immediately.

Bruce Speck
President, 2008 to present
Missouri Southern State University (Joplin, Missouri)
Carnegie Classification: Public; 4-year or above; Baccalaureate Colleges—Diverse Fields
5,264 Students
In September 2009, the faculty senate brought a list of concerns with Speck's leadership to the school's board of governors. The concerns included repeated turnover in school leaders, an adversarial shared governance relationship, cuts to the school's Institute of International Studies, and instances when Speck displayed questionable judgment in public. The faculty also voted no confidence in Speck's leadership.

The board of governors issued a statement directing Speck to improve faculty relations. He remains president of Missouri Southern State University.

Brian Johnson
President, 2007 to 2009
Montgomery College (Rockville, Maryland)
Carnegie Classification: Public; 2-year; Associate's—Public Suburban-serving Multicampus
24,452 Students
Faculty leaders raised concerns that Johnson was often absent from campus, missed important meetings, and used his university credit card for personal purchases. In September 2009, the faculty voted no confidence in President Johnson; the trustees placed him on paid leave the following week. He resigned under a negotiated separation agreement in December 2009. The settlement terms are confidential.

Bob Kerrey
President, 2001 to 2011
The New School (New York, New York)
Carnegie Classification: Private not-for-profit; 4-year or above; Doctoral/Research Universities
9,825 Students
Faculty and student leaders criticized Kerrey for high administrative turnover, politically unpopular statements, secrecy, and prioritizing fiscal concerns over academics. After his fourth provost in seven years left, Kerrey announced that he would take over the provost's responsibilities. In response, the faculty held a no-confidence vote, which Kerrey lost 271-8. At the same time, student protesters staged a two-day sit-in calling for his resignation. In April 2009, a second sit-in ended when student protesters were arrested.

Kerrey left his post on January 1, 2011, at the end of his contract term.

James Oblinger
Chancellor, 2005 to 2009
North Carolina State University at Raleigh (Raleigh, North Carolina)
Carnegie Classification: Public; 4-year or above; Research Universities (very high research activity)
32,872 Students
In 2005, former North Carolina First Lady Mary Easley was hired into a newly created position at NCSU. In 2008, she received an 88 percent pay raise. A federal grand jury has been convened to determine whether her hiring was illegal. Interim provost Larry Nielson and a trustee, who were responsible for Easley's hiring, resigned, citing the intense public scrutiny.

Chancellor Oblinger released a series of contradictory statements regarding the terms of Nielson's severance before resigning suddenly in early June 2009. Oblinger has not been accused of any wrongdoing.

Joseph Chapman
President, 1999 to 2009
North Dakota State University (Fargo, North Dakota)
Carnegie Classification: Public; 4-year or above; Research Universities (very high research activity)
13,230 Students
Chapman announced in October 2009 that he would resign from NDSU after ten years at its helm. He had been recently criticized for cost overruns of more than $1 million on his home construction, having his wife on the payroll of the NDSU Development Foundation, and spending $22,000 in university funds to attend President Obama's inauguration.

Bob Richburg
President, 1987 to 2009
Northwest Florida State College (Niceville, Florida)
Carnegie Classification: Public; 4-year or above; Associate's—Public 4-year Primarily Associate's
7,463 Students
In 2007, State Representative Ray Sansom arranged for approximately $6 million to be allocated to construction of a "multi-use educational facility" at Northwest Florida State College. The facility was to be built by one of Sansom's major contributors, and the school's vice president in charge of facilities was not aware of the project until after the money had been approved. Sansom was subsequently hired into a high-paying job at the college.

In April 2009, Richburg and Sansom were indicted on felony charges of misconduct and perjury. Richburg was immediately placed on leave and was fired the following week.

Clarence Newsome
President, 2003 to 2009
Shaw University (Raleigh, North Carolina)
Carnegie Classification: Private not-for-profit; 4-year or above; Baccalaureate Colleges—Diverse Fields
2,703 Students
In May 2009, Newsome announced that he would resign. Shaw University was more than $20 million in debt, had cut faculty pay, and had suspended retirement benefits. Students staged protests about pest-ridden dorm facilities and moldy classrooms, and trustees announced that they would each contribute $50,000 to support the school.

A confidential agreement with the trustees terminated Newsome's contract with a one-year paid sabbatical and undisclosed benefits.

Ralph Slaughter
President, 2006 to 2009
Southern University System (Louisiana)
Public University System
5 Schools
13,733 Students

In 2007, the board of supervisors suspended Slaughter. He filed a whistleblower lawsuit claiming his suspension was in retaliation for reporting that a former board member had sexually harassed female university employees. The board cleared the former member of wrongdoing and settled Slaughter's lawsuit.

In April of 2009, the board voted Slaughter's job performance satisfactory but indicated that they would not renew his contract when it expired. He filed three lawsuits claiming the board had violated open meetings laws when it met to vote on his contract. After negotiations with the board, he agreed to drop the lawsuits. Slaughter finished his contract term on June 30, 2009, and has since filed additional lawsuits against the school.

Harold Raveché
President, 1988 to 2010
Stevens Institute of Technology (Hoboken, New Jersey)
Carnegie Classification: Private not-for-profit; 4-year or above; Research Universities (high research activity)
5,595 Students

As of 2008, Raveché's contract gave him more than $1 million in compensation annually. In September 2009, the New Jersey attorney general filed a sixteen-count complaint against the university, some members of the board of trustees, and Raveché. Charges included mismanagement of the university's endowment, deliberately withholding information from some board members, and overpaying the president. The complaint also alleged breach of fiduciary obligation. Indicted board members were accused of misrepresenting committee work to the board at large and spending more than twice the legally allowed amount from the university's endowment. In 2005, PricewaterhouseCoopers had dropped SIT as a client because it was too great a liability; members of the board's audit committee reported to the board that the firm had simply stopped taking nonprofit clients. Raveché was accused of receiving excessive compensation, including low-interest loans, many of which were eventually illegally forgiven.

Stevens settled the lawsuit by agreeing to substantial changes in its governance structures and other financial oversight measures. Under the terms of the settlement, Raveché resigned June 30, 2010, but was paid his salary for another year and will continue to serve in the capacity of paid consultant through 2014. Raveché will repay the illegal loans.

Elsa Murano
President, 2007 to 2009
Texas A&M (College Station, Texas)
Carnegie Classification: Public; 4-year or above; Research Universities (high research activity)
48,039 Students
The Texas A&M System Chancellor, Michael McKinney recommended Murano for the job; the shared governance search committee did not. Press reports indicate that she gradually developed support among faculty and students, although most of the senior administrators at the school were replaced during her tenure. After her first year, McKinney's review of Murano's performance was harshly critical. He indicated that she did not comply with system directives and was too reliant on shared governance. Murano responded with a written rebuttal, sent to the entire board of regents, claiming that McKinney undermined her authority. Murano resigned in June 2009 when it became clear that the board of regents was about to vote to fire her.

Public speculation focused on the political dimensions of the conflict. McKinney is a former aide to Texas governor Rick Perry, who also appointed all of the system regents. McKinney has suggested that the president's responsibilities could be subsumed into his position as system chancellor. Early in her administration, Murano was criticized by faculty for bowing to pressure from McKinney and Perry to hire one of Perry's college roommates as the vice president of student affairs. In contrast, she angered McKinney by conducting a national search for the vice president for research position. The search committee declined to recommend a Perry associate for the job; McKinney hired that individual into a newly created position at the system level.

Stephen Jennings
President, 2001 to 2010
University of Evansville (Evansville, Indiana)
Carnegie Classification: Private not-for-profit; 4-year or above; Master's Colleges and Universities (smaller programs)
2,742 Students
In 2008, Jennings was arrested for drunk driving. He apologized to the community and enrolled in a rehabilitation program. Trustees released a statement supporting Jennings.

Jennings retired from the University of Evansville on May 31, 2010. It is unclear whether his retirement decision was related to the drunk driving incident.

B. Joseph White
President, 2005 to 2009
University of Illinois System
Public University System
43,246 Students
In May, press reports suggested that University of Illinois applicants with political connections were receiving special treatment. Records later released by the school indicated that ap-

plicants with influential supporters were considered separately, and, in some cases, admitted over other, more-qualified applicants.

Over the summer of 2009, six members of the board of trustees were replaced, and, in September, President White resigned. He remains at the University of Illinois as a business professor.

Philip Williams
President, 2006 to 2010
University of Montevallo (Montevallo, Alabama)
Carnegie Classification: Public; 4-year or above; Master's Colleges and Universities (medium programs)
3,023 Students
Williams agreed to a compromise that allowed another university to establish a satellite campus near Montevallo. In exchange, that university did not object to Montevallo's new MBA program. Trustees were unaware of the deal, and some objected that they had not been consulted.

When Williams's contract was up for extension in August 2009, he publicly announced that he would resign if he did not receive the full support of the board of trustees. The board responded by placing Williams on a four-month sabbatical.

After a mediation process with the board, Williams announced he would return to work, but resigned effective July 31, 2010. The chairman of the board of trustees resigned at the same time.

David Ashley
President, 2006 to 2009
University of Nevada–Las Vegas (Las Vegas, Nevada)
Carnegie Classification: Public; 4-year or above; Research Universities (high research activity)
28,600 Students
Ashley publicly clashed with James Rogers, the chancellor of the University of Nevada system, who accused Ashley of absentee leadership and alienating an important alumni group. Ashley's wife was also criticized for treating university staff poorly; she publicly apologized and announced that she would no longer act as a hostess on behalf of the university until her role was clarified. Rogers had also publicly clashed with Nevada's governor and with Carol Hartner, the previous president.

In June 2009, Rogers publicly announced that Ashley's contract was unlikely to be renewed. Regents subsequently voted to remove Ashley from his post. He remains at UNLV as a professor of engineering, earning his presidential salary, through the end of his contract. Rogers left the board at the end of July 2009.

David Schmidly
President, 2007 to present
University of New Mexico System
Public University System
5 Schools
25,754 Students
In 2008, a study revealed that executive compensation had increased 71 percent in six years. Schmidly responded by announcing cuts to administrative spending and a freeze on all executive salaries.

Schmidly's son Brian was offered a $94,000 job at the university. After faculty complaints, Brian Schmidly declined the job. President Schmidly denied any involvement in the hiring decision, and a university investigation found that he had not been involved.

In February 2009, the faculty voted no confidence in President Schmidly, David Harris, the university's CFO, and James Koch, the president of the board of regents. Faculty also called for an audit of expenditures. Schmidly remains president of the University of New Mexico.

John Petersen
President, 2004 to 2009
University of Tennessee System
Public University System
5 Schools
47,791 Students
In February 2009, Petersen abruptly announced he would resign. Trustees were in the midst of conducting a five-year performance review. Although he had received a positive annual review earlier in the year, Petersen had been criticized for financial difficulties and for a public clash between his wife and a prominent donor. In addition, the chancellor of the Knoxville campus resigned in 2008 after a public dispute with Petersen.

Blandina Cardenas
President, 2004 to 2009
University of Texas–Pan American (Edinburg, Texas)
Carnegie Classification: Public; 4-year or above; Master's Colleges and Universities (larger programs)
17,534 Students
In 2007, auditors found that Cardenas had improperly used $7,000 in university funds; she reimbursed the university.

In 2008, an anonymous packet was sent to school leaders and media, alleging that Cardenas had plagiarized her dissertation. The university launched an investigation, which was halted in January of 2009, when Cardenas announced she would be retiring from her post, citing health reasons.

Rev. Julio Giulietti
President, 2007 to 2009
Wheeling Jesuit University (Wheeling, West Virginia)
Carnegie Classification: Private not-for-profit; 4-year or above; Baccalaureate Colleges—
Diverse Fields
1,319 Students
From the beginning, Wheeling Jesuit University's board of directors was split over Giulietti's
hiring. In August 2009, the board of directors held a vote on whether to fire Giulietti, but
they failed to reach the required two-thirds majority. A separate board of trustees, comprised
entirely of Jesuit clergy, then convened and voted to overrule the board of directors. It is unclear whether the trustees had the authority to fire Giulietti, but, following the second vote,
one of Giulietti's superiors in the Jesuit order asked him to resign.

Neither the board of directors nor the board of trustees gave any reason for Giulietti's
ouster. Public speculation has explored several possibilities, including a critical report from
NASA's inspector general over mismanagement of federal funds, personality conflicts with
prominent board members, and a property dispute with the local bishop over the future of a
convent adjacent to WJU.

Bibliography

American Association of Community Colleges. "2013 Community College Fact Sheet." www
.aacc.nche.edu/AboutCC/Pages/fastfactfactsheet.aspx.

American Council on Education, Center for Policy Analysis. *The American College President*.
Pennsylvania State University, State College, PA: American Council on Education, 2007.

Association of Governing Boards. *Effective Governing Boards: A Guide for Members of Governing
Boards of Public Colleges, Universities, and Systems*. Washington, DC: Association of Governing Boards, 2009.

Bentz, V. J. "A View from the Top: A Thirty Year Perspective on Research Devoted to Discovery,
Description, and Prediction of Executive Behavior." Paper presented to the annual conven-
tion of the American Psychological Association, Los Angeles, CA, 1985.

Bogue, E. Grady. "Political Ping Pong: The Constructive Uses of Conflict." In *Leadership Legacy
Moments*, by E. Grady Bogue. Westport, CT: ACE/Praeger, 2007.

Burns, James MacGregor. *Leadership*. New York: Harper & Row, 1989.

Ciulla, Joanne B. "Ethics and Leadership Effectiveness." In *The Nature of Leadership*, edited
by J. Antonakis, A. T. Cianciolo, and R. J. Sternberg, 302–327. Thousand Oaks, CA: Sage
Publications, Inc., 2004.

Collins, Jim. *Good to Great*. New York: HarperCollins, 2001.

De Pree, Max. *Leadership Is an Art*. New York: Doubleday, 1989.

de Vise, Daniel. "Eight Scandals That Ended College Presidencies," *Washington Post*, Local Section, November 21, 2011.

Drucker, Peter F. *The Effective Executive: The Definitive Guide to Getting the Right Things Done*.
New York: Harper and Row, 1967.

Fain, Paul. "In Apparent Suicide, Chancellor Dies in a Fall." *Chronicle of Higher Education*, July
7, 2006, 1.

Feinberg, Mortimer, and John J. Tarrant. *Why Smart People Do Dumb Things*. New York: Fire-
side, 1995.

Fiedler, Fred E. *A Theory of Leadership Effectiveness*. McGraw-Hill, 1967.

Foreman, Alison. "Lack of Board's Support Prompts Bennett President to Resign." *Diverse Education*, February 14, 2002.

Gentry, W., J. Hanum, B. Ekelund, and A. deJong. "A Study of the Discrepancy between Self and
Observer Ratings on Managerial Derailment Characteristics of European Managers." *European Journal of Work and Organizational Psychology* 16, no. 3 (2007): 295–325.

Greenleaf, Robert K., and Larry C. Spears. *Servant Leadership: A Journey into the Nature of Legitimate Power and Greatness.* Mahwah, NJ: Paulist Press, 1977.

Harel, Elazar C., and Toby D. Sitko. "Digital Dashboards: Driving Higher Education Decisions." *Educause Research Bulletin*, September 16, 2003, 19.

Hesselbein, Frances. *Hesselbein on Leadership.* San Francisco, CA: Jossey-Bass, 2002.

Koestenbaum, Peter. *Leadership: The Inner Side of Greatness.* San Francisco, CA: Jossey-Bass, 1991.

Leslie, J. B., and E. Van Velsor. *A Look at Derailment Today: North America and Europe.* Greensboro, NC: Center for Creative Leadership, 1996.

Lombardo, M. M., and C. D. McCauley. *The Dynamics of Management Derailment* (Tech. Rep. No. 34). Greensboro, NC: Center for Creative Leadership, 1988.

Lubker, John R. "Using a Case Study to Hire a Dean." *Chronicle of Higher Education*, September 2011.

MacTaggart, Terrence. *Leading Change: How Boards and Presidents Build Exceptional Academic Institutions.* Washington, DC: Association of Governing Boards, 2011.

Masterson, K. "U. of Illinois President Resigns in Wake of Admissions Scandal." *Chronicle of Higher Education*, September 23, 2009.

McCall, M., and M. Lombardo. "What Makes the Top Executive?" *Psychology Today* 17, no. 2(1983): 26–31.

Morrison, Ann M., R. P. White, E. Van Velsor, and the Center for Creative Leadership. *Breaking the Glass Ceiling.* New York: Addison-Wesley, 1987.

Robie, Chet, Douglas J. Brown, and Paul R. Bly. "Relationship between Major Personality Traits and Managerial Performance: Moderating Effects of Derailing Traits." *International Journal of Management*, 25, no. 1 (2008): 131–139.

Shaw, Robert Bruce, and Michael M. Chayes. "Moving Up: Ten Questions for Leadership in Transition." *Leader to Leader,* Winter 2011, 39–45.

Trachtenberg, Stephen Joel. "Not What It's Cracked Up To Be," *New Directions in Higher Education,* December 1981, 3–9.

Walker, Donald E. *The Effective Administrator: A Practical Approach to Problem Solving, Decision Making, and Campus Leadership.* San Francisco, CA: Jossey-Bass, 1979.

Contributors

Stephen Joel Trachtenberg is University Professor of Public Service and president emeritus of the George Washington University, after serving nineteen years as president of the university. He arrived at GW in 1998 from the University of Hartford where he served as president for eleven years. Prior to that, he was at Boston University for eight years, as dean of arts and sciences and vice president. He is a fellow of the American Academy of Arts and Sciences and a member of Phi Beta Kappa and of the Council on Foreign Relations. Professor Trachtenberg is the Chairman of the Higher Education Practice at Korn/Ferry International. He lives in Washington, D.C.

Gerald B. Kauvar is the special assistant to the president emeritus and research professor of public policy and public administration at the Trachtenberg School of George Washington University. He has served as a faculty member at the University of Illinois, City College of New York, and the George Washington University. He also served as a special assistant to three university presidents and was a senior executive in the Department of Defense from which he retired as the special assistant to the secretary of the Air Force. He was staff director for the White House Commission on Aviation Safety and Security and worked at RAND as a senior policy analyst. He has published books and articles on English and American literature, psychoanalysis, homeland security, higher education, and management.

Before his death in 2013, *E. Grady Bogue* was Professor of Leadership and Policy Studies at the University of Tennessee, chancellor emeritus of Louisiana State University in Shreveport, where he served for eleven years, and former interim chancellor of Louisiana State University and A & M College in Baton Rouge. He served in a variety of leadership roles at campus and state levels, as a consultant to colleges, state level agencies and corporations, and as an officer in the United States Air Force, and was a distinguished alumnus of the University of Memphis.

Bogue published ten previous books on leadership and quality and accountability themes and more than sixty articles in journals such as the *Harvard Business Review, Leader to Leader, Journal of Higher Education, Trusteeship, Educational Record, Phi Delta Kappan,* and *Planning for Higher Education*. Bogue's interests included playing the French horn. He was married to the former Linda Young and was father of five children.

Keith Carver is the executive assistant to the president of the University of Tennessee. Prior to this, Carver served in various administrative positions at the University of Tennessee at Knoxville. He holds two degrees from the University of Tennessee, Knoxville (MS '95, PhD '09). An avid reader, runner, and fisherman, Keith lives in Knoxville with his wife, Hollianne, their daughter, Carson, and their sons Jack Thomas and Britton.

Julie Longmire earned her PhD in higher education administration from the University of Tennessee as well as a master's degree in college student personnel studies. She currently serves as the assistant director of career services at Lincoln Memorial University–Duncan School of Law and has served as site coordinator for the Lincoln Memorial University–Cedar Bluff Extended Learning Site. Prior to that, she served as coordinator of undergraduate advising at the University of Tennessee College of Education, Health, and Human Sciences. In her spare time, she enjoys traveling, practicing kenpo karate, and spending time with her family.

With fifteen years of higher education leadership experience, *Jason McNeal* is a consultant with Gonser Gerber, North America's most innovative advancement consulting firm. He serves clients in the United States and Canada, providing presidents, boards, and advancement leaders with personalized counsel in the areas of strategic planning, board relations, and fundraising. Prior to joining Gonser Gerber, Jason served as the chief advancement officer for two higher education institutions. Jason's blog, www.jasonmcneal.com, is devoted to helping higher education leaders operate strategically and engage donors and other key constituents in the work of the enterprise. A graduate of Salisbury University in Maryland, Jason completed Harvard University's Higher Education Management Development Institute, and earned a PhD degree in higher education administration from the University of Tennessee. He lives with his wife, Heather, and two children—Shelby and Sam—in Maryville, Tennessee.

Leigh Anne Touzeau earned her PhD in higher education administration from the University of Tennessee as well as a master's degree in college student personnel. She currently serves as the assistant vice president of enrollment services at Pellissippi State Community College in Knoxville, Tennessee. She has twenty years of work experience in higher education and has held positions in residence life, career services, admissions, and orientation. She has worked at private and public universities but the majority of her experience has been in the community college sector. In her spare time, she enjoys traveling, reading, and spending time with her family.

Index

academic enterprise, 2–3, 56, 105

adaptation, difficulty in, 7, 8, 9, 13–14, 59, 130; to academic presidencies, ix; at community colleges, 67–69; to community culture, ix, 14, 67–68; to institutional culture, ix, 14, 39, 56–58, 67–68; at private liberal arts colleges, 30–31; at public master's level universities, 36, 37–40; at public research universities, 57–58

alcohol, 27, 72, 73, 74, 108

alumni, 26, 40, 46, 112, 118, 126

American Association of Collegiate Registrars and Admission Officers, 87

American Association of Community Colleges, 60

American Association of University Professors, 41

Association of Governing Boards of Universities and Colleges, 116

athletic programs, 50, 52, 58, 84, 85; and Garrison, 80, 81, 84–85, 91

Bennett College, 10

Berendzen, Richard, 76

Beychock, Shelley, 134

board chairs: autocratic, 117; as cheerleaders and overseers, 128; and communication, 106; and conflicts of interest, 33, 100, 117; ethics oversight by, 54; factual information from, 127; focus on policy and strategy by, 127; and Frawley, 79; and fundraising, 127; and Garrison, 83, 84, 86–90; inspirational, 127; manipulation of, 32, 117; as model for board members, 128; ongoing feedback from, 126–27; and performance evaluation, 127; at private liberal arts colleges, 28; replacement of supportive, 45; role of, 127–28; and Sullivan, 111, 112; timely provision of materials by, 117, 127; traits of unsuccessful, 127–28; and transparency and accountability, 127; weak or imperial, 115

board members, ix; accountability of, 139; alienation of, 26; attendance and preparation by, 117; board chair as model for, 128; communication with, 128; leadership of, ix; performance of tasks by, 127; at private liberal arts colleges, 26; reelection of, 116

boards, 139; administrative decisions by, 16, 63, 105; aloof, 62–64; appointment of, 44; assessment of, 99–100; authority of, 45, 117; and Bogue, 134; and boundaries of presidential authority, 45; breaches of confidentiality by, 8; and broader social and civic interests, 133; as cabal, 116; changes in membership of, 44–45; and characteristics sought in candidates, 103; communication with, 32–34, 40, 99, 105–6, 110, 116, 118, 128; at community colleges, 61–68, 70; and conflicts of interest, x, 8, 15, 16, 33, 100, 115, 117, 130; consideration of termination by, 114–15; core responsibilities of, 105; costs of derailment to, 6–7; as creating conditions for success, 115; and dashboards, 126; disclosure of information to, 25; dismissiveness toward, 41; divided, 8, 32, 43, 56; dual loyalties of, 92; as duplicitous, 115, 132; duties of committees of, 116; dynamics of, 111–28; ethical oversight by, 53; ethics of, 33, 34, 100, 115, 117; executive committees of, 32, 116, 126–27; experience of, 130; and factionalism, 116; and faculty,

boards (*cont.*)
100; fiduciary responsibility of, 105, 113; and Frawley, 74–76, 79–80, 91; funding of personal hobbyhorses by, 115; and Garrison, 82–91; governance role of, 63; and government representatives, 64, 70; and governor, 39, 44, 133; and group dynamics, 116; hiring and firing by, 1, 44, 113; independent meetings with students, faculty, and staff by, 115; and institutional culture, 58, 68, 113, 115, 120; and institutional strategy vs. tactics, 113; and institution's long-term interests, 131; and institution's priorities, 116, 117; as key constituency, 44–45; lack of strong relationships with, 66–67; leadership of, ix, 44–45, 130; management of campus anxieties by, 120; meddling in administrative decisions by, 15, 16; and membership on other boards, 106; micromanagement by, 8, 63, 70, 115, 117, 130; misreading of, 8; open, inclusive work of, 116; as overlooking character flaws, 116; as overpowering, 63; and performance reviews, 32–33, 123–25; policy oversight by, 105; and political meddling in search, 130–31; and political system, 44; and politics, 132, 133; as premier among stakeholders, 131; preparation and attendance of, 127; at private liberal arts colleges, 22, 23, 25, 26, 29–33; at public master's level universities, 38, 40, 41, 43–45; at public research universities, 53–56; reconnection with institutional stakeholders by, 121; responsibilities of, viii, 1, 16, 34; retreat by, 121; risk mitigation by, 130; and searches, 16, 43, 53, 99–101, 105, 109–10, 114, 130–31, 138–39; self-examination by, 121, 138; and shared governance, 113, 117; shortcomings of, x, 8, 9, 15–16, 31–33, 44, 53–55, 92, 100, 116, 130; and strategic goals, 105, 113, 115, 116; and strategic planning, 105, 113, 115, 116, 127, 128; and Sullivan, 111–13; as swayed by faculty, 66–67, 70; and transition periods, 14, 34; transition planning by, 119–23, 138; unified support from, 44; and unity around institution's priorities, 116, 117; and unity in appointment after search, 109; weak over-

sight by, 8; working relationship with, 12, 13
Bogue, E. Grady, 134–35
budget, 117–18; and Garrison, 83; poor management of, 48; and private liberal arts colleges, 24, 26; and public master's level universities, 39, 48; and transition period, 122. *See also* finances
Burns, James MacGregor, *Leadership,* 16
business objectives, x, 8, 9, 23–27, 29, 130

cabinet, of senior staff, 128; communication with, 25, 40; failed guidance of, 42–43; and Garrison, 83; as ignored, 47; inability to lead, 130; inexperienced, 41, 42, 52, 55; lack of counsel from, 55–56; leadership of, ix, 12; letters of resignation from, 135–36; and private liberal arts colleges, 25; and public master's level universities, 36, 40, 42–44, 47; and public research universities, 52, 55; responsibility of, viii
Cade, John, 134–35
change: at community colleges, 62, 65, 68–69; faculty involvement in, 68–69; and Garrison, 81–84, 89, 90, 91; inclusion of board in, 118; and institutional culture, 57, 58; and long-term planning, 132; open discussion and debate of, 38; organizational, 38, 40, 42, 52, 57, 58, 62; pace of, 14; at private liberal arts colleges, 28, 29, 32; at public master's level universities, 38, 42; at public research universities, 52; resistance to, 52; and Sullivan, 112
Churchill, Winston, 113
Ciulla, Joanne B., "Ethics and Leadership Effectiveness," 4, 10
Cole, Jonathan, 105
Collins, Althea, 10
Collins, Jim, *Good to Great,* 11
communication, ix, 104; with boards, 32–34, 40, 99, 105, 106, 110, 116, 118, 128; ineffective styles of, 7; lack of, 25, 38, 40; lack of skill in, 43; lack of transparent, 24; and poor listening, 47; and private liberal arts colleges, 25; and public master's level universities, 37, 38, 40, 46, 47, 49; and University of Virginia, 113; of vision, 63

community: and community colleges, 61, 65;
disagreement with, 46; involvement with,
105; as key constituency, 46; and private
liberal arts colleges, 26, 30; and public
master's level universities, 35, 37–41, 46; and
town-gown relations, 39, 46, 65, 84
community colleges, 60–70
community culture, 26; adaptation to, ix, 14,
67–68; and private liberal arts colleges,
27–28; and public master's level universities,
46; of surrounding community, 26
conflicts of interest, x, 8, 15, 16, 33, 115, 117. *See
also* ethics
contracts, presidential, 79–80, 98, 119, 124, 139
credit rating agencies, 23

dashboards, 125–26, 127
DeFleur, Lois B., 5
Denton, Denice, 10
De Pree, Max: *Leadership Is an Art*, 12, 136–37
derailment, vii; costs of, 1, 5–7, 114; defined,
vii, 1, 9
Dobelle, Evan, 92, 113
donors, 6, 40, 46, 48, 83, 84, 91, 112
Drucker, Peter, *The Effective Executive*, 2

ethics, viii, 1, 5, 59, 129; and arrogance, 138;
and background checks, 54; and boards, 8,
33, 34, 115, 117; cost of lapses in, 10–11; and
disclosure of information, 25; and Frawley,
92; and hiring of family members, 10, 65,
115, 117; immediate address of, 7; and leadership, 137; and leadership effectiveness, 4;
of predecessors, 54; in public master's level
universities cases, 37, 39, 47–48; in public research universities cases, 51–53; and search
process, 110; as theme, ix, 5, 8, 9. *See also*
conflicts of interest

faculty, 50; board as swayed by, 66–67, 70; and
boards, 100; and change mandates, 68–69;
at community colleges, 61, 62, 65–68;
disregarded input of, 42; fractured and
warring, 8; and Garrison, 81–83, 86, 88, 89,
91; inability to lead, 130; and institutional
culture, 68; lack of communication with,

40; leadership of, ix; misreading of, 8; poor
relationships with, 36, 40, 41–42, 117; at
private liberal arts colleges, 26, 29, 30; and
public master's level universities, 36, 38–42,
47; and public research universities, 50; and
reorganizations, 40; on search committees,
101; skills relating to, 56, 57; and University
of Virginia, 112; working relationship with,
12, 13
Fallon, John, 76
family: hiring of, 10, 65, 115, 117; of president,
73, 76, 92, 98, 105, 106
Fiedler, Fred, *A Theory of Leadership Effectiveness*, 15
finances, 15, 105, 126; audits of, 55; disclosure
to search candidates of, 99; irresponsible
management of, 47; lack of communication
about, 24; and private liberal arts colleges,
24; and public master's level universities, 39,
47; and resources diverted for personal use,
54–55. *See also* budget; funding
Fogel, Dan, 5
Frawley, William, 71–80, 91
Freud, Sigmund, 138
funding, 39, 45, 48, 54–55, 63–64. *See also*
finances
fundraising, 23–26, 41, 105, 127

Garrison, Michael, 71, 80–91, 92
George Washington University, 72, 73
governance, 2, 3, 98, 113, 131; and boards, 117;
and consensus building, 2, 38, 40, 48, 56–57;
and public master's level universities, 38, 41;
and public research universities, 50; shared,
41–42, 98, 113, 117
government: and boards, 64, 70; and community colleges, 61–64; contentious relationships with, 37; inability to lead, 130; as
key constituency, 45; leadership of, ix; and
private liberal arts colleges, 26; working relationship with, 12, 13. *See also* legislatures;
state system
governors: and boards, 39, 44, 133; and Bogue,
134; ethical oversight by, 54; and Garrison,
88; meddling in search by, 131; and public
master's level universities, 39, 40; and Uni-

versity of Virginia, 112–13; working relationship with, 12, 13
Greenleaf, Robert K., *Servant-Leadership*, 11

Herman, Richard, 10
Hesselbein, Frances, *Hesselbein on Leadership*,
10
honesty, 39, 47, 48, 73, 76–79
Hoover, Robert A., 92

institutions, culture and context of, 7–8, 104;
adaptation to, ix, 14, 39, 56–58, 67–68; and
boards, 58, 68, 113, 115–17, 120, 131; and candidate's previous assignments, 110; of community colleges, 63; and Garrison, 81; and
inexperienced cabinet, 55; and mission and
vision for future, 121; and private liberal arts
colleges, 30–31; and public master's level
universities, 37, 38, 48; and public research
universities, 57–58; understanding of, 8, 137
interpersonal skills, 1, 4, 7, 59, 104, 128, 129;
and aggressiveness, 65; and anger, 24, 25,
29, 30, 43, 46, 126; and arrogance, viii, 11,
38, 54, 64, 69–70; and authoritarian style,
29, 41–42; and communicativeness, 37;
in community colleges cases, 62, 64, 65,
68–70; and contentiousness, 43, 44, 46–47,
65; cultivation of, 136; defined, ix, 11–12;
and demeaning manner, 69–70; and formal-
ity, 27–28; and leading key constituents, 12;
and merit of honest dissent, 56; in private
liberal arts colleges cases, 24, 25, 27–31, 34;
problems with, 8, 9; in public master's level
universities cases, 37, 38, 41–44, 46–49; in
public research universities cases, 54, 56–57;
and secretiveness, 29

Kauvar, Gerald B., 72
Kerr, Clark, 17
Koestenbaum, Peter, *Leadership*, 15

Ladner, Benjamin, 76
Lariviere, Richard, 5
leaders, 8; as defining reality, 137; effectiveness
of, 2–4; gratitude of, 137; and interpersonal
skills, 11; of key constituencies, ix; legacies
of, 16–17; styles of, 104, 110

legislatures, 37, 40, 41, 44, 103, 131, 133. *See also*
government
Louisiana State University Shreveport, 134–35

MacTaggart, Terrence, *Leading Change*, 13
media, 17, 39, 46, 114; and Frawley, 75–76, 91,
92; and Garrison, 88–91; training for, 122
mission, 37, 39, 48, 50, 122, 131. *See also* planning, strategic
Moody's, 23

Northwestern State University, Natchitoches,
134, 135

performance reviews, 32–33, 34, 90–91, 106,
112, 123–25, 127, 139
personal life, 105–6
planning, strategic, 15, 72, 76; and boards, 105,
113, 115, 116, 127, 128; and cost of derailment, 6; and institutional progress, 23; and
key stakeholders, 128; and transitions, 122.
See also mission
predecessors, 14, 34, 117; and community colleges, 62, 66, 67; differences from, 120–21;
ethical lapses of, 54; presence of, 32; and
private liberal arts colleges, 26, 28, 29; and
public research universities, 52, 54; rituals
for departure of, 120
private liberal arts colleges, 21–34
public master's level universities, 35–49
public research universities, 50–59

racial discrimination, 41
Reagan, Ronald, 17
religion, 26–29, 131
Rodriguez, Rich, 80, 81, 84–85, 89, 91
Rosen, Jeffrey, *The Unwanted Gaze*, 73

searches, viii, 8, 59, 93, 97–110; appointment
of committee for, 100–101; background
check in, 43, 53, 54, 108–10; and boards, 16,
43, 53, 99–101, 105, 109–10, 114, 130–31,
138–39; and candidate credentials, 138; and
candidate's past accomplishments, 98; and
candidate's psychic makeup, 138–39; and
candidates' public persona, 109; characteristics sought in, 99, 102–4, 107; communica-

tion of finances, strengths, and operating challenges in, 99, 110; cronyism in, 110; and Garrison, 81–82; and gossip/hearsay from previous institution, 106–7; group think in, 107; honest public announcements about, 97–98; imprecision of, 97–98; inattention to concerns expressed in, 55; and institutional needs, 105, 107; and integrity of process, 138; internal candidates in, 107–8; job description for, 102–3; lack of unanimous support in, 56; manipulation of, 16; openness and transparency in, 138; pitfalls of, 109–10; politics in, 130–31; procedural requirements in, 107; professional guidance and support for, 99, 101–2; and public master's level universities, 43; and public research universities, 53–56; screening in, 99, 106–9; as selective in appointing search committee, 99; shared information and mutual expectations for, 99, 105–6; and stakeholders, 15, 101, 131, 138; unity about appointment in, 99, 109

search firms, ix, 101–2

sexual misbehavior, viii, 10, 52–53, 76, 138

Shaw, George Bernard, 70

Silber, John, 5

Spanier, Graham, 5

Spilman Thomas & Battle, 80

staff, 26, 57, 83, 89, 91, 101

stakeholders/constituencies, ix, 12–13, 70, 131; ability to relate to, 110; balancing interests of, 131–32; board as premier among, 131; and characteristics sought in candidates, 103; at community colleges, 61–67; diversity of academic, 12; and Frawley, 91; and Garrison, 83, 91; inability to lead, 8, 9, 129–30; loss of confidence of, 48; as multiple, 55, 56, 64–66, 101; and performance evaluations, 124; personal meetings with, 136; at private liberal arts colleges, 26–31; and public master's level universities, 36, 40–46, 49; and public research universities, 50, 55–56; relationships with, 34, 128; and searches, 15, 101, 131, 138; and strategic planning, 128; and University of Virginia, 113; working relationships with, 12

Standard & Poor's Financial Services, 23

state system, 37, 39–40. *See also* government

strategic direction, 105, 112

students: admission of, 38; applications of, 126; and dashboards, 126; enrollment of, 15, 23, 24, 26; and Garrison, 82; at private liberal arts colleges, 23, 24, 26, 30; and public master's level universities, 35, 37–38; retention of, 15, 24, 126; and search committees membership, 101; and University of Virginia, 112

Sullivan, Teresa, 111–13

teaching, 21, 35

Trachtenberg, Stephen Joel, 72; "Not What It's Cracked Up to Be," 97

transitions, 93; and budget, 122; ceremonial farewells and welcoming festivities in, 120; and communication by board, 34; desire for expedient, 54; and Garrison, 82–83; interpersonal relationships during, 29; ongoing nature of, 120, 121; planning of, 119–23, 138; at private liberal arts colleges, 29; and public master's level universities, 37; and public research universities, 54; as refreshing moment of opportunity, 120, 121; self-examination by board during, 121; and strategic planning, 122; support during, 14

Treen, Dave, 134, 135

University of Delaware, 72

University of Hawaii, 113

University of Mary Washington, 71–77. *See also* Frawley, William

University of Virginia, 111–13

vendor contracts, viii, 33

Walker, Donald, 11

West Virginia Higher Education Policy Commission, 80, 81

West Virginia University, 80–91. *See also* Garrison, Michael

White, Joseph, 10

Wise, Bob, 80, 81

Woods, Dalton, 134–35